TRAVELS WITH A
KAYAK

Vanning the globe to bring you . . .

the spill of victory* and . . .

*Not to mention the hand that cradles the rock

the agony of the feet. It's . . .

TRAVELS WITH A
KAYAK

Whit Deschner

THE EDDIE TERN PRESS

[Joe Potter photo]

Acknowledgment is made to the British Canoe Union for permission to reprint from the *BCU Canoeing Handbook* (1981), and *BCU Guide to the Waterways of the British Isles* (1961).

Various portions of this book appeared in various forms in these various publications: *Canoeist, Currents, Canoe, Paddler,* and *Northwest Wilderness Journal.*

Some of this book is fiction, other parts originated with non-fiction facts that I made up. Certain characters are total fabrications and purely fictional. Anyone mentioned in this book who does not wish to sue me for libel is real; those who feel otherwise should address their suits to courts of fictional law. Please note that if your face appears in one of the photos in this book, it is now copyrighted; however you have my permission for its continual usage.

This book is a special, limited 500-run edition of which this is number **18654**. The paper on which it is printed is carefully hand-selected steamrolled turkey gizzards, guaranteed to last several millennia, providing the book is not left out in the sun for long periods. The pages have been carefully numbered so when ripped apart, the book can be easily glued back together in numerical order.

PHOTOS: Page 2 top to bottom; Frank Cranbourne, Frank Cranbourne, Frank Soll, Whit Deschner. All other photos, unless indicated, are by Whit Deschner's altered ego, Bill Harzia.

Proceeds from this book go directly to myself, Whit Deschner, a non-profit organization.

Cover design and book layout by Elizabeth Watson
Edited by Candace O'Connor
Maps by Marge Mueller, Gray Mouse Graphics
Photo work by Baker City Photo, Dick and Rella Browne

Library of Congress Cataloging-in-Publication Date:
    Deschner, Whit, 1901-
    ISBN# 0-9605388-6-0
    1. Whitewater Kayaking 2. Travel 3. Humor
    4. Questionable Tax Write-offs.

97-90587
CIP

Printed in Canada

To my parents, Tom and Laura Deschner, [second and third from bottom] who introduced me to kayaking in the mistaken belief that it would keep me out of trouble.

And to Carol, who made sure I stayed there.

Cast of Characters

Greystoke a.k.a. Dan Dixon

Green Slime a.k.a. Peter Knowles

Since the following people appear in more than one of the stories, I'd like to introduce them here so as not to have to do so continually throughout the text. I met Carol Haslett in 1979 while boating in the Northwest. Without her many of my subsequent exploits would not have happened—like the trips I was talking about in 1982 (A.D.) in Vancouver (B.C.), where I was giving a slide show and where my life was about to be consigned to the tyranny of happenstance: I met Dave Manby. He advised me that in my ensuing travels I should keep a lookout for a friend of his, Green Slime, a.k.a. Peter Knowles . . . Three years later coincidence led to our meeting in Lhasa. And in Kathmandu Slime introduced me to (among others) Dan Dixon, a.k.a. Greystoke, one phenomenal boater. Several years later I led a trip into B.C. and both Dave Manby and Greystoke tagged along. The year after, Dave organized a trip to Turkey that had on board both Slime and Greystoke. The following year, Slime organized his trip to Pakistan, where I met Andy Watt. Subsequently Andy and Dave hopped on a Grand Canyon trip that Carol organized. Later, Carol and I met up with Andy in India, where he was practicing medicine in Manali, and together we boated the Spiti.

Along with the above, others, too, were of tremendous help along the way. Without them, this book would not have been possible. Therefore any complaints about the book should be addressed to the following:

Dave Allardice, Anne Appleby, Craig

Andy Watt, the "all-touristic" doctor

Bagdasar, Bill and Gerri Baldwin, Peter Bani, the Baron River Canoe Club, Mary Ellen Benson, Greg Bristow, George and Dorothy Bodgan, Arlene Burns, Clyde and Jenny Cook, Frank Cranbourne, Larry Davidson, Matt Deschner, Sue and Collin Eades, Rick and Cheryl Ewings, Joe and Marquita Green, Ken and Angie Green, Mark Haslett, Jill Hodgshon, Dave and Sue Horrocks, S. Igarashi, Ward and Lois Irwin, Milt Jines, Jerry Johnson, Wayne Jordan, Payson Kennedy, George Kosen, Rob Lesser, George and Verna Lewis, S. Scot Litke, Peter and Elwyn Lynn, Ted Mattson, Goodwin and Mary McNutt, Gerry Moffat, Pete Montgomery, Bruce and Joan Morrison, Cameron O'Connor, Roger Palmer, John and Ali Quirk, Dave Reed and Krysia Carter-Geiz, Tim and Joanna Simcock, Richard and Denise Tait, the Tokyo Canoe Club, Diane Troje, Bob Tyler, Stuart Wagstaff, the Washington Kayak Club, John Watson, Royce Ward, Ron Watters, and Don Weeden.

Dave Manby, organizer of world-wide chaos

. . . . a smaller boat, for one man . . . covered completely over, except a hole in which the occupant sits, and around the projecting rim of which, when at sea, he ties the edge of a waterproof skirt, called a kamláyka *by the Russians. This is securely tied around the wrists and face also; the head being covered by a hood, so that no water can by any means penetrate to the interior of the boat. This boat is called by the natives a* kýak *. . . .*
—William H. Dall, *Alaska and its Resources,* 1870

Conditions of Success and Failure in Travel.—An exploring expedition is daily exposed to a succession of accidents, any one of which might be fatal to its further progress. The cattle may at any time stray, die, or be stolen; water may not be reached, and they may perish; one or more of the men may become seriously ill, or the party may be attacked by natives . . .
—Francis Galton, *Art of Travel,* 1872

This devious course had taken the boat to several different kingdoms and states—Holland, Belgium, France, Wurtemburg, Bavaria, and the Grand Duchy of Baden, Rhenish Prussia, the Palatinate, Switzerland, and the pretty Hohenzollern Sigmaringen. Now we had come back again to the very Grand Duchy again, a land wherein all travellers must mind their p's and q's.
—John MacGregor, *A Thousand Miles in the Rob Roy Canoe,* 1881

Water Table of Contents

A note to non-boating readers
[as opposed to non-reading boaters]

River classification covers a broad range from class or grade 1—a sluggish, monotonous flow with zero obstacles—to class 7 requiring funeral arrangements to be in order. Although at times the rivers in this book seemed much harder, most of the water described is class 3 and 4.

"Holes" are caused by water pouring over a ledge or rock creating a horizontal backwash. Due to their vigorous recycling programs, large holes should be avoided at all costs—as should the people who purposely go into them.

"Endos" or **"end-over-ends"** are merely a fancy way of tipping over—vertically.

"A Shuttle" is the clever art of having transportation both to and from the river—with a minimum of hassle. Although rarely as spectacular as river-running itself, shuttles are usually far more life-threatening.

"cfs" stands for cubic feet per second.

◀ Class 2. Circa—1963 boater Jean Morris on the circa—1963 Satsop, Washington. [c,—1963 Harry Burlingame photo]
▶ An "endo" or end-over-end.

Class 5. Lance Young, Canyon Creek, Washington.

Preface

The first liar never stands a chance.

—*American proverb*

Around 1968, when I began boating, I saw Bruce Brown's classic surf movie, *The Endless Summer*. Although I was not (and am not) a Californian, do not have blue eyes and blond hair (or today blue hair), the movie made such a lasting impression on me that eight years later I was on my way to New Zealand to paddle its rivers with the granddaddy of big water paddling, Walt Blackadar. Although the experience didn't always exceed my expectations, it did, at least, tickle them. More notably, though, the trip spawned in me the desire to see additional pieces of the world by kayak. For reasons I can't fathom, I began to write about these trips.

And for even deeper, unknown reasons I began submitting these articles, picking especially on Britain's *Canoeist* magazine, where, to the total bewilderment of its readers—and detriment of its subscriptions—many of these pieces first appeared. This was arranged, at great sacrifice to his career, by Stuart Fisher, who runs the show, and who, if he had not printed them, would probably be on a par with Rupert Murdoch right now. So I thank him profusely for giving his readers something different; in return, his readers occasionally wrote back letters of praise—well, for example, like this one:

> *I read with utter amazement the immature and childish article written by Whit Deschner on kayaking and rafting down the Grand Canyon. Having read it several times in case I was missing the point I became more incensed with the comments he made regarding his trip:....*

And there are plenty more where that came from; however, space and modesty prevent me from sharing them. But allow me a few short words of introduction to these pieces. Historically, river-runners have never quite told the truth. Whether whitewater just does this to people (something in the water?) or it is a wrong turn in the DNA maps is unknown. Take, for example, Major John Wesley Powell. Saturating his Grand Canyon account (which was really two trips) with half-truths, while liberally adding extra height to the rapids, he wanted the public to believe he had done the impossible, wrongly assuming no one could ever follow in his wake. Or glance at Walt Blackadar's encounter with the Alsec: He claimed its gorge was unpaddlable. I'll quit there, not wanting to offend anyone currently living who makes a buck off such tales— like myself. Not that I wish to start matching chromosomes with other river-yarn fabricators; I just want to make clear that my humble accounts make no effort to deviate from what has become a well-trodden path.

What you are about to read, or perhaps throw away, are stories where fiction and fact live recklessly in sin together. Despite what it seems, I did not write these pieces with a faulty memory, but rather adjusted them for the cruel injustice of circumstance, embellishing events that by my denied rights, should have happened, omitting at the same time trifles that refused to fit the mold of debonair adventure writing. Besides, as an unsuspecting—but bloodthirsty—reader, you probably do not realize that, in order to sell writing to an adventurous, travel-oriented market today, an author has to have at least several people die per trip.[1] Let this book then not disappoint you. *At least five or six people perish per article.* On some of these trips the participants met slow, tragic deaths. Difficult decisions had to be made and, for the assurance of a sale, they were left behind to die. On other trips, four or five people were indiscriminately killed off just to reach the "sensational article quota." This was too bad and all of that. However, despite the epic proportions of these trips, not once did the surviving members go hungry, due to the extra rations these tragedies provided.[2]

I also wish to preempt any criticism (what little there might be) of the book. A foreign reader might ask, "What's the big idea of going all around the world making fun of other people and hardly saying anything about the U.S.?"[3] Well, let me inform you: We here in the U.S. are not in the least bit concerned about trite issues such as overpopulation and destruction of our natural environment. We discuss loftier issues like Elvis sightings and blue M&M's. The same questioning foreigner who visits my place might inquire, "Why, I just counted thirty-one bullet holes in the road sign nearest to your house. Is a revolution going on here?" And I would reply, "No, that's our way of life . . . ." A way of life that surrounds me with religious nuts and political zealots. Just to give you an idea of the caliber of people I am talking about, take the following true-life story. My neighborhood is plagued by frequent drive-by shootings. This is because I own one of the most ground squirrel-infested alfalfa fields within two zip codes. Once, confronting one of these squirrel assassins, I said, "I'd appreciate it if you wouldn't shoot my squirrels, since I've got horses in the field beyond." This person stared at me as if I had three heads and said, "Don't you think I can tell the difference between a ground squirrel and a horse?" Not only do we let such people breed in this country, we let them run for office.

But enough! As I dismount from my high horse before it crashes through this thin ice, allow me one last comment. Through the years I mistakenly thought that kayaking, in the U.S. and abroad, was offering me an escape from becoming a mundane and warped human being. I was wrong. It merely provided me a window to see things in yet another distorted, misconstrued manner. These are my stories.

---

[1] Have you ever seen a picture of the same person going over two different waterfalls? Of course not. They never live past the first one.

[2] No, not cannibalism.

[3] While a U.S. reader might ask, "Is English *really* your native language?"

Introduction

Dë Sçĥñér on Kayaking:
In One Era and Out the Other

My clothes for this tour consisted of a complete suit of grey flannel for use in the boat, and another suit of light but ordinary dress for shore work and Sundays.

The "Norfolk jacket" is a loose frock-coat, like a blouse, with shoulder-straps, and belted at the waist, and garnished by six pockets. With this excellent new-fashioned coat, a something in each of its pockets and a cambridge straw hat, canvas wading shoes, blue spectacles, a waterproof overcoat, and my spare jib for a sun shawl, there was sure to be a full day's enjoyment in defiance of rain or sun, deeps or shallows, hunger or ennui.

—John MacGregor, A Thousand Miles in the Rob Roy Canoe, 1881

At the end of the summer I had begun to make a kayak for a single man, the frame of which was of bamboo carefully lashed together. It was rather slow work, and took several weeks, but it turned out both light and strong. When completed the frame-work weighed 16 lbs. It was afterwards covered with sail-cloth by Sverdrup and Blessing, when the whole boat weighed 30 lbs. . . . These kayaks were 12 feet long, about 28 inches wide in the middle, and was 15 inches deep.

—Fridtjof Nansen, Farthest North, 1898

The other day I realized how much older I am getting when a kid stopped me and asked what kayaking was like "in the old days." He had fuzz on his face that I'd call a down payment on a beard, water dripped from behind his ears, and the word "neophyte" was tattooed across his forehead.

I said, "What do you mean by old days?"

"Like twenty-five years ago, before it was popular or profitable."

I should have slugged him. But then I realized that in the world of kayaking, even five years can be several geological time periods. So I began my litany.

For starters, the rivers we boated then were much bigger. I know they were, as a documented fact, for in every one of my slides, the kayaker is no larger than a dust speck. In fact, if you actually want to discern a kayaker in one of these slides, you have to use a magnifying glass, not a slide projector.

People gaze tongue-tied at my slides and—when their speech returns—exclaim, "Why look at the size of that river! And that kayaker! It makes him look like a dust speck!"

I have to correct them, "That *is* a dust speck. *There's* the kayaker!"

I have no explanation for this larger-then phenomenon. However, I have noticed a peculiar pattern. My pictures prove that rivers were colossal when I started kayaking and have progressively shrunk ever since. When I began, rivers were *so* big, that my newly purchased camera didn't even pick up the kayakers I was trying to capture on film. Twenty-seven years later, my pictures of kayakers are so overwhelming they usually blot out the river. People admiring these shots often say, "Look at those dust specks!"

And I correct them, "Those aren't dust specks. Those are zits!"

Conditions were also colder then. In fact, we used the Kelvin scale, since the temperatures when we were boating failed to reach even the lower ends of the Fahrenheit or Celsius scales. Hypothermia would often set in immediately—and this was before we reached our river. While we were putting chains on, a conversation along these lines would frequently ensue:

Bob: "You are having an affair with my girlfriend!"

Bill: "I am not!"

Bob: "Denial! The first signs of hypothermia."

Bob to the rest: "Bill's hypothermic!"

Bill: "I do not have hypothermia!"

[Page 16] Kayaking before it was neither popular or profitable. In the 50s boats were of a folding nature so they could be secretly stashed in the trunks of cars. With them being hidden there was little concern for social embarrassment while driving down the highways. Today, many people, including non-boaters, bolt kayaks onto their roof racks merely to enhance their image. [Tom Deschner photo]

Bob: "You do!"
Bill: "Do not!"
Bob: "Do!"

And so on—until the unavoidable fight warmed everyone back up.

On the river, evidence of hypothermia was easier to ascertain: the blue lips, the glazed eyes, rigor mortis—quickly followed by the victim's companions going through his wallet and divvying up his boating gear. In those days we didn't have the luxury of swarms of boaters tipping over, their body heat warming the waters.

We used to wear what were known as *wetsuits*—something now banned in every state except Nevada and New Jersey. We bought them at sex shops. They were called wetsuits because they were always wet—that is, unless they were frozen. No one ever successfully dried one between trips; those who tried eventually checked into mental institutions. The theory of wetsuits was that your personal body heat would warm the water inside the suit, insulating you from the cold, (I'm not mentioning the zipperless models, when the wearer had consumed gallons of coffee). But really it was more like a carpenter saying to himself each morning, "Well since I'm going to be hammering nails today, I might as well just smash my thumb and get it over with!" Actually, the way wetsuits worked was that they emitted such a strong stench it overpowered all sense of cold the wearer felt. Even after the wetsuit was removed—and burned—the wearer's skin was thoroughly marinated with a smell that not even a steam cleaner could remove.

Unfortunately, this presented socially embarrassing situations, like returning from river trips hungry and wanting to stop at a cafe for a bite to eat. If we were waited on, it was usually in some vacant lot adjacent to the establishment where the waitress approached us wearing a gas mask. The food was inevitably accompanied by a note asking us never under any circumstance to return.

Sometimes it was just beer we sought. Whoever was volunteered for this job would stuff his pockets with Limburger cheese in a feeble attempt to camouflage the smell and then enter a store. Nine times out of ten they would emerge empty-handed, pursued by an irate manager waving an Uzi.

It was the notion of drinking beer after river trips that brought up an ill-fated plan conceived by—I shall refer to him as Pete, since that was his name. Our group had just put in a hard day on a

The Washington Kayak Club, spring 1957, Middle Fork Snoqualimie River. [Tom Deschner photo]

A typical boating scene in the 70s.

local run and had worked up a powerful thirst. Pete's blockheaded idea was to slip into a biker's bar while still in our wetsuits. In such a dingy and low-class dive it would be—so the theory went—impossible to tell the difference between leather and rubber. Together, we must have smelled like a large animal lathered in sweat, rolled in a manure pile, and dead three weeks. However you describe the smell, it offended the bikers. But it turns out that the wetsuits did have a redeeming factor; they cushioned the impact to our reeking bodies as the bikers attempted in vain to fuse human flesh with pavement. It was a pity Pete had not thought of wearing helmets. I know for a fact that I've never again encountered a group of such evil-spirited women.

The other attribute of wetsuits was that they protected the wearer from fiberglass, a derivative of itching powder used to make kayaks. A kayaker who was fool enough not to shield himself with a wetsuit, went home scratching and tearing at himself as if a troop of famished fleas was trying to eat through not only a heartbreaking case of psoriasis, but a seven-year itch as well.

Kayaks in those days were not as they are today; the anti-gravity wonder that a thirty-pound weakling can toss, one-handed, into the trunk of his car. They were spine-fusing boats that took at least four people and three hernias to lift onto and from a roof rack. (Roof racks actually went on top of cars, in the days when cars had gutters.) These kayaks were designed with the lines of the *Exxon Valdez* in mind, and holed just as easily when they collided with rocks, reefs, and other oil tankers.

This necessitated patching boats, an innocent activity at first. A group of friends stood around a damaged kayak passing a resin container, inhaling large whiffs and giggling hysterically. But it was a dangerous business and quickly led to more sinister habits, like boat building.

I was lucky not to have hit too many rocks and not to have gotten hooked. I was fortunate that I did not degenerate into a boat builder with enough intelligence to carry on long, meaningful conversations with such people as Ronald Reagan or Muhammad Ali. For example, here's an actual conversation between two boat builders:

Tom:

John:

Tom:

John:

Boats were not something you wore. Their most important feature was storage space for the cases of duct tape one needed for temporary repairs made below each rapid. Up front there was more leg room than in five Japanese cars combined. Any favorable effect this had on a boat's maneuverability was purely coincidental. We were not concerned with being able to hang in a boat upside down; we never tipped over. Those who were fool enough to do such a thing certainly did not have to worry about a complicated escape route, so long as all the multitudes of salmon in the river weren't hampering the effort.

Paddles, then, were simply paddles. They weren't made from a NASA by-product or twisted into half-a-dozen geometric shapes that required a triple-jointed contortionist to use them. Paddles were either left-feathered, no-feathered, or right-feathered. Anyone who showed up for a trip with left- or no-feathered blades was never asked on a trip again, since their paddle did not fit on a roof rack with the rest of the paddles.

As far as color went, there wasn't any. At that time, kayaking was not socially acceptable or politically correct. In fact, it was one of the few sports that was available to the homeless, as I myself was then. So you certainly didn't wish to be zealously enthusiastic about outfits with color. Today, thanks to the work of lunatic manufacturers, color is splashed over life jackets and helmets and drysuits with such abandon that boaters look like they are impersonating Las Vegas at night. Few realize how color first crept into the sport. It was accidentally introduced by a color-blind person.

Unfortunately, the first day I decided to try color was also the day I trespassed into Seattle's watershed for a first descent of the Cedar. I donned a flaming red paddle jacket; it was so loud that it hurt the eardrums. I completed the run—and the watershed personnel completed their arrest of me. After they chased me the entire way down river, the red they were seeing was not just on my paddle jacket.

Finally, I wish to point out that it was not *us* who named the rapids. Long after all the rivers had been run in the western U.S., there were two commercial rafters who went around and named everything. Although they were both typical rafters, they differed in their interests: one was toilet oriented; the other a Satan worshipper. Thus, until the next large meteorite hits the planet, we are stuck with names like "Toilet Bowl," "Devil's Pinball," and "Satan's Flush."

In those days, our system of names was far superior. We didn't have to use such concrete, base references. We just used to say things like, "You mean the rapid where Joe cracked his helmet yesterday?"

"No, not that one."

"Oh! Where John dislocated his shoulder!"

"Yesterday?"

"No, you're thinking of the place where Mike wrenched his back. *I'm* talking about that place Mary got pinned."

"Oh, that one!"

But I digress. Over the years, I suppose the sport has actually changed for the better. I'd like to see it. In fact, right now I'm going to pull my boat out of the back yard, mix up a little resin, and fix some of the bigger holes that I know are still there from the boat's last use—twenty years ago. Ahhh, that smell! I feel better already!

NEW ZEALAND

Part I: With Walt

*The kyaks are often ornamented with beluga teeth, or carved pieces
of walrus ivory, imitations of birds, walrus, or seal. The prow is
also fashioned into the semblance of a bird's or fish's head. Securely
seated in his kyak, with a gut shirt strongly tied around the edge of
the hole, the Innuit is at home. He will even turn over his kyak and
come up on the other side, by skilful use of his paddle.*

—William H. Dall, *Alaska and its Resources*, 1870

❖   ❖   ❖

As any Kiwi will insist upon telling you, New Zealand is a harmless
little country—just so long as you don't berth on the *Rainbow
Warrior* in the Auckland Harbor, or get buried under lava and hot ash
from one of the country's volcanoes, or get shaken to death in an earthquake, or boiled in a geyser, or washed away in a rainstorm, or die of
starvation trying to hitchhike from the West Coast, or get poisoned by
radiation from French nuclear testing—you'll be fine. And, save for one
teeny-weeny poisonous spider that only bites tourists, even the animals
are harmless. Just don't mention the gaping hole that sheep flatulence is
ripping in the ozone which will, by the year 2012, cause every earth occupant to be fried to death like sun-roasted ants under a magnifying glass.
Never, ever say anything negative about sheep. And whatever you do, do
not discuss *Silence of the Lambs*.

Sheep are to New Zealand what cows are to India. Leading economic
indicators are given in sheep; the stock market index is read off in units of

Walt Blackadar on the road to the Shotover. Of the two roads on which we were specifically not to drive our rental car, this was one of them.

sheep. Even the common idioms are sheep-oriented—like "having the wool pulled over your eyes" by the government and "being fleeced" at tax time. This sheep-reverence baffles tourists when they first arrive. Customs agents do not ask, "Are you bringing in tons of illegal drugs?" or "Do you have any highly contagious fatal disease, such as ebola or black plague?" No, worried about their sheep contracting hoof and mouth disease, they inquire, "Have you been on a farm or know anyone who has been on a farm or have you spoken to anyone who has been on a farm in the last three years?"

Say yes and you are packaged off like a drug smuggler in Singapore and are never heard from again. Say no and you are allowed to claim your luggage—dripping, of course, from the sheep dip it was just rinsed in.

Unfortunately, the three that made up our party—Walt Blackadar,[1] R.F., and myself—said no and were allowed to pass Go. I say unfortunately because I had only known R.F. for the duration of the flight over and I was already hoping that misfortune would befall him. R.F. was an acquaintance of Walt's, an heir to enough money to buy the entire U.S. House of Representatives. Just as we boarded the plane in San Francisco and Walt and I were herded off into steerage, R.F. asked what kind of kayak I had. I said I owned

[1] Born August 13, 1922. Drowned May 13, 1978, South Fork Payette River.

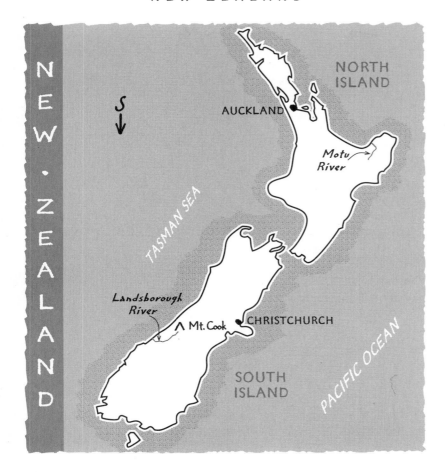

several and R.F. replied—as three blond stewardesses ushered him into the First Class section—"Well *I* own twelve oil tankers."

Walt, I didn't really know, but I had boated with him once in April 1974, on Idaho's St. Joe river. He was short and stocky with Ernest Borgnine eyebrows; I don't know what I expected a well-known kayak personality to look like, but this was hardly my composite picture of one. Cute, female, and my age would have been more like it.

What was impressive about Walt was his kayak, a $400 epoxy Lettman. Epoxy, the miracle plastic of the day, was only affordable by the rich and famous, and anyone who worked with it became a drooling invalid within six months. The boats of us ground-level insects were polyester, costing a third as much. Walt's paddle, an

Iliad, roughly measured out to the surface area of Kansas. Dumping with an Iliad, if you were lucky enough to get the blade to the surface, meant that either one of two things happened: You would roll up so fast you'd have whiplash or, if not, every joint in your shoulder would be permanently dislocated in trying.

That day in Idaho, Walt was eager; snow lined the river, and when he headed for the water with his boat someone said, "What the hell's he want to go and do that for?" From the pseudo-security of a van with its heater inadequately blowing full blast, we watched Walt snuggle into his boat, purposely tip over one way, roll, tip the other, and roll. Then, as he headed downstream, a half dozen of us, feeling guilty, made a dash for the river and started off after him.

Descending, Walt hardly turned into an eddy. In one place the river swept around a corner which everyone except Walt cheated on the inside. Not only did he pursue a more difficult route he did so upside down. He rolled several times on his right side and, while he did so, a discussion took place in the eddy.

Someone #1 said: "He always runs rivers like that."

Someone #2 argued: "No one in their right mind runs rivers *like that* unless it's a warm day."

And Someone #3 added: "Well I bet those eyebrows keep him from getting ice cream headaches."

I thought, "Surely he's got to know another stroke."

It came at Tumble-down Falls: a broken dog leg with dual folding waves that hit in a left-blindside-right combination, dumping everyone. Here, Walt employed his other stroke: a roll on the left—which was better than the side-stroke the rest of us used swimming to shore.

So I only knew Walt from the St. Joe. Later, hearing he wanted to go to New Zealand, I gave him a call, asking if I could tag along.

"Sure," Walt said, "But can you me do a favor?"

I said I would.

"Will you organize the trip?"

The three of us were unlikely traveling companions. Walt treated me like a son and R.F. treated me like baggage. I suspected this because often he'd say to Walt, "Is the baggage coming?" and "Where are you and the baggage going to stay tonight?"

He asked this latter question each evening as Walt and I dropped him off at whatever hotel rated the most stars in town. Among R.F.'s mound of luggage were pillows in three sizes. Big was devoted to hotel use because, even in luxury hotels, the pillows were not suitable. Medium was for camping, something R.F. loathed. Economy was for rivers, should we—God forbid— overnight on one. So Walt and I would camp without R.F., while he went and found a real bed on which to put his real pillow to lay his real swollen head on.

We drove south, which, when you start from the north, is the only thing you can do in New Zealand. Although the country is a thousand miles long, it is only fifty feet wide: Travel east or west and you're immediately in an ocean.

Overall, with the exception of its place names, New Zealand is primarily an English-speaking country. I choked on place names laughing: Porroporro, Paki Paki, Murumuru, Whanawhana, Hakahaka, Matakitaki, Matukituki, etc. etc. They were not like the good solid place names where I come from: Humptulips, Dosewallops, Stilliquamish, Tumtum, Walla Walla, etc. etc.

As we traveled we got to know the people, along with their strange, twisted sense of national achievement. They eagerly reminded us about Hillary and Everest, but within the same breath, went on to inform us that the Hamilton Jet is a creation of Kiwi ingenuity. They think it's a big deal that Hillary climbed some

Project raft flip on the Matukituki— not the Matakitaki.

geologic freak in the Himalayas, but look at what jet skis have done for the enhancement of civilization! Of course, both these accomplishments pale in comparison to their most successful claim to fame: the kiwi fruit. To take advantage of sexually bored American housewives no longer tempted by mushy red delicious apples, the Kiwis realized they would have to develop a fruit so titillating that even Eve would have fallen from grace at terminal velocity had she seen one. Subjecting Chinese gooseberries to steroids, they came up with an egg-shaped fruit covered with a adolescent facial hair. Sliced open, it evinces the exciting semblance of bile. This fruit, the Kiwis like to boast, quickly became the essential ingredient of their national dessert, Pavlova, a dish so famous the Russians named a ballerina after it.

At a party we were served this dessert and it was there where Walt distinguished himself in American diplomacy. Now Walt was a good guy and all that, but he could have used a few more tips in international refinement. After several helpings of Pavlova, washed down liberally with vodka, Walt launched into one of his favorite attention-grabbing topics: breasts. Unfortunately he didn't say, "You should have seen the udders on that ewe!"—which is a perfectly acceptable party subject in New Zealand. Instead, standing, he offered a toast to all the breasts in the room and announced that if the women didn't like them he could surgically alter them any way they desired. Judging by the pin-drop silence and the room full of flushed faces, bust overhaul was not a subject openly discussed in this society.

◆　◆　◆

We drove some more. I'd gaze at the scenery whizzing past and say, "The heir's sure getting stuffy in here!"—and R.F. would roll down his window. What I really wanted him to do was open his door and jump out. However, this would have caused problems, because R.F. was always driving. Walt didn't want to drive and R.F. didn't want my caste getting in the front seat with him, which was fine with me. I sat behind him and used him as an heir bag.

The first piece of whitewater we saw was Huka Falls, a thirty-foot drop. Walt, speaking in R.F.'s direction, said he would run it for five thousand bucks but R.F., Patron Saint of millionaire tightwads, didn't make the connection. (The falls were run six years

later by Greg Oakes and Nick Kirkam who, not wanting to damage their own kayaks, used two club boats that were specifically not to be used on anything over a class 2.)

Sheep dotted the region around the falls and I thought, there's got to be something abnormal about a sheep-fixated society. When we arrived at our first river, the Tongoriro, a questionable farmer tried selling us a sheep for questionable purposes. At first, I thought he was on the level. Four bucks he wanted.

"What do we do with it?" R.F. asked.

The farmer said, "Anything you want." Then I began wondering as I watched R.F.'s eyes widen.

I figured Walt would instantly squelch such a perverse offer, but instead he entertained it. "Four dollars. That's incredible! Do you know how much a live sheep costs in Salmon?"[2]

I had no idea this sort of thing went on in Salmon but I said nothing. I thought I had possibly misinterpreted the situation, but then I knew I hadn't when the farmer added, "Give me eight and I'll dress it for you."

"What do you say?" Walt asked us.

"Forget the sheep," I whispered back to him. "Ask if he'll take four bucks and give us the clothes."

We ran the lower Tongiroro, a delightful run but not half as delightful as the Maori kids we floated past. Assuming we were

[2] Idaho. One of the few remaining salmon in that state.

somehow related to Captain Cook, these self-appointed juvenile delinquents began showering us with rocks. R.F. paddled towards them and began screaming angrily, "YOU KIDS STOP THROWING . . . "

But he never finished. A bulls-eye boinked him right on the helmet.

After one river in one disappointing week on the North Island, we crossed Cook Strait to New Zealand's Significant Other and dawdled some more until Ashburton. There we met boater Clyde Cook who promptly introduced us to Vegemite, a culinary disaster made from concentrated sheep's droppings. Vegemite, as we were to learn, is considered the pinnacle of New Zealand gastronomy, which is about the equivalent of a Floridian bragging about the highest mountain in his state. Even the most caustic stomach acids won't digest Vegemite and its smell alone is capable of terrorizing the Tokyo subway system. In fact, Amnesty International lists it as a major crime against humanity.

Walt Blackadar in his element running an unrun drop on the Rangitata, not to be confused with the Rangitaiki or the Rangitikei.

After trying to poison us, Clyde produced a map and showed us the un-run Landsborough, a river that flowed southward from Mt. Cook. Quickly, the four of us made plans and the following day traveled to the West Coast, where we learned about the region: It has more rain drops per square inch than water in the Pacific Ocean, and it is the only place in the country where the number of sheep is superseded by the number of sandflies—airborne cannibals that make mosquitoes look like tooth fairies. When bad weather is not obscuring the Southern Alps, swarms of sandflies are. However, don't get me wrong about the West Coast: it's a nice place to live— if you like terrariums.

Now Walt, Clyde, and I thought the Landsborough map's contour lines supplied adequate information but R.F. insisted on first chartering a plane to scout the river. Walt said, "Fine, as long as you pay for it." The aerial view told us exactly what the map had.

After landing, R.F. leaned over and whispered in my ear, "Hope you liked the free ride."

I said nothing but I must have been turning several different colors in anger when Walt asked, "What's the matter with you?"

"Nothing," I answered, "I'm just feeling a little heir-sickness."

Because of giving up a day to R.F.'s sightseeing, we lost our window of good weather. Nor was our helicopter pilot enthusiastic about our plans. He was pessimistic about the weather, pessimistic about what his copter could carry, and pessimistic about the whole scheme in general.

Over the next three days—at R.F.'s insistence—the pilot attempted to fly us in. Both times we were turned back by cloud cover and finally we had to call it quits. R.F. temporarily disappeared while I paid the bill.

R.F. left the following day, but not before I had reminded him he still owed me for his share of the helicopter. He informed me we were now even: he'd paid for the plane and I'd paid for the helicopter. Then he drove away. Watching the rental car recede into the distance I wrote his epitaph:

R.F.

Millionaire skinflint.
His charm and manner and unfailing kindness always
endeared him to all who knew him.

Walt and I kicked around the idea of still running the river, but the weather voted otherwise. So we did the only thing you *can* do in New Zealand: traveled further south, boated, saw the sights and lost large quantities of blood to sandflies.

We spent five minutes in Milford Sound, a large rock alley filled with water and tour boats.[3] We turned around and almost passed up the upper Hollyford and *should* have, but didn't. It was a steep run and littered with a housing development of cottage-sized boulders, but there was little volume, allowing plenty of time for jockeying through the neighborhood. Easements became increasingly restricted and portages common; while we were portaging, the sandflies eagerly began unzipping our wetsuits to get at some fresh meat.

Finally we came to a small, walled-in area and the drop facing us, T-boned, doubtful accommodation for a boat's passage. The portage promised to devolve us into quadrupeds. I told Walt I'd climb up and look for the road. It was an easy walk out and when I returned, I applied some basic kayak humor: "There's no escape." I informed him, "We've got to run this one."

He didn't question me or even climb up to gain a perspective on the drop. He was simply going to forge on even though the route seemed impossible. It's the incident I have always remembered him by.

That evening, after our walk out, Walt made arrangements for returning to the States and I called our helicopter pilot, asking if I could work in exchange for being flown into the Landsborough.

"Why, sure!" he said, bubbling with optimism.

Only when Walt dropped me off and wished me luck did I learn the reason for the pilot's excessive cheer. He said, "I don't think you're going to make it!" Then he added, grinning, "The government will pay me handsomely to fetch your remains."

Four days later, as the pilot unlashed my kayak from the skid, he said, "If you're not out in five days, I'll come looking for you." Wanting to duplicate Walt's notorious, lone, self-described suicidal Alsec run, I had made this arrangement, too. I liked to hear the pilot say it because it made for high drama, one of the essential elements in a saleable magazine article. But after being sand-blasted by the departing helicopter, and watching it disappear quickly through the cloud of sandflies encircling me, I said to myself, "Fine mess I'm in now." Although my vision was blinded by the

[3] It reminded me of what an old Norwegian once told me, that his government had let the fjords get overrun by Finnish tourists.

"What's that supposed to mean?" I asked.

"That the Fin is mightier than the fjord."

sandflies, the real reason the river had not been run became startling clear: No one had been dumb enough to sacrifice themselves to these flying Draculas. At that very moment, the sandfly-to-human ratio in the valley was exactly six jillion to one. Quickly, I got into my boat.

In an article I subsequently wrote on the descent, the term "adrenalin" appeared 57 times, "near death" 36, and my heart beat underwent more rate increases than monthly insurance premiums. I described water as "angry" (23 times), "frothing" (15), "vicious" (11), and "upheaving" (5). Other passages of note were: ". . . surrounded by jagged mountains, the only gap in the horizon was to the south, cut by the river . . . rendered the gorge below unmanageable . . . continuous rapids . . . occasional dim ray of evening sun penetrated the bottom of the gorge . . . swirled in whirlpools and cauliflowering upheavals rebelling against impending banks . . . river suddenly disappearing in front of me . . . big rough water . . . main current dumped itself into a rock-clogged jumble . . . percolating the water . . . six-foot tongue plunging into a mushrooming reversal . . . no more eddies to escape into . . . committed . . . water gushing through the disarrangement of boulders . . . into a wall of turbulence . . . I gasped for a last breath . . . buried and stopped me . . . bivouac . . . no longer thinking rationally . . . current stacked up against a truck-size rock dead center in the river . . . maze of boulders . . ."

And all this happened within the first fifty feet.

It took me two days to come out. Yet if I thought the river was challenging, it was nothing compared to getting away from it. In my haste to pack, I'd forgotten my clothes. It took me two days to hitchhike—with my kayak—cross-country to Ashburton. All I was wearing was my wetsuit, and upon my arrival the town was evacuated.

Not much happened over the next month except I wound up under house arrest for overstaying my visa. Of course it wasn't my fault. The blame lay with two Danish nurses who spirited me away to Stewart Island and insisted on hiking a full circuit of the island—in the nude. In the meantime, Clyde, noting my disappearance and recognizing opportunity when he saw it, contacted the police, who quickly gave me up as both dead and missing. That allowed Clyde's conscience to clear about what he'd done with my equipment: He'd sold it.

Part II: Why I am Not a Guide
(The Landsborough)

Drowning.—To Excite Respiration. Turn the patient well and instantly on his side, and excite the nostrils with snuff, the throat with a feather, and dash cold water on the face previously rubbed warm . . .

—Francis Galton, *Art of Travel*, 1872

◆ ◆ ◆

Four years later I returned to New Zealand, this time with what I thought was a promising future. Since I had already observed Clyde's business-sense, we set up a little travel concern together: I was a whitewater guide. Little did I know. Not only was my next two weeks of guiding one of the shortest stints ever recorded in the annals of the business, it was also the longest two weeks of my life. Somehow I thought being a guide would be different, that the lone question I would be required to answer would be: "Can I buy you another drink?"

But there was none of that. This group wanted to know trivial, annoying things like, "What's downstream?" and "*How* hard did you say this river was?"

I had hoped Clyde could answer these questions, but when such questions were asked, Clyde was nowhere around. He was off running the shuttle because, he explained, it was very complicated. So complicated that he'd often be sound asleep when we arrived.

The trip might have even turned a profit if it hadn't been for one small glitch: Clyde. Clyde had booked us into the most expensive hotels he could find. "How come?" I asked.

"Because I'll never get a chance to stay in them again and neither will you, so stop complaining."

Any hope at all for profit lay in selling our boats after the trip, but the clients quickly began devaluing them in every way their

Back for more punishment; arriving to run the Landsborough a second time.

little boat-destroying minds could imagine. In the early evenings, the only luxury Clyde and I enjoyed at his hotels were the double-mowed lawns in the rose gardens. There, much to the hotel management's chagrin, we set up our fiberglass shop repairing boats and draped our boating gear on the rose bushes to dry.

Five days into the trip, I was dealt another blow. I had lost a three-way bet with Clyde and a client, and the loser had to wear nothing but a spraydeck to a party at the Palmerston North Canoe Club. Fortunately, it turned out to be a costume party. Unfortunately, as a joke, my ride left early and I was forced to traverse Palmerston North at two in the morning in nothing but my costume. Dodging behind various hedges and into people's yards with each oncoming car, I thanked my lucky stars that the police's attention was never called to my existence.

After ten years of premature aging compressed into ten days, we finally arrived at the Landsborough, the river where my expertise would be needed. Regrettably, neither Clyde nor I had taken into account that the copter trip into the Landsborough seemed to have gotten longer—and more expensive—over the last four years, destroying any prayer we had left for profit. Trying to keep out of the red, we took another route over the mountains, putting in just upstream from where I'd put in before. It was a pleasant put-in, the river harmlessly meandering through a pastoral meadow. And when we climbed into our boats, the clients discovered that I wasn't temporarily deaf after all; that I didn't have a severe shoulder twitch that looked suspiciously like a shrug every time they asked me something about rapids. Everything went fine for two-hundred yards. Then the river disappeared.

"Huh," I said. "River's changed a bit since I was here last."

Yet the closer I drifted to the horizon line, the more it remained a horizon line.

"Funny thing, this," I said. "Didn't seem to be much trouble running it last time. Never even got out of my boat. But just in case, why don't we take a look."

The portaging took seven hours.

"Look at the bright side," I reminded Clyde as we abseiled down yet another cliff. "Think of the money we saved."

"Yes, but you think you'll be allowed to live so you can spend it?"

That night, out of rock-throwing distance from the clients, I assured them all was well, that we were past the hard part. The next morning, I correlated our position on the map, showing my charting from my run before. "Harmless as a kitten today," I affirmed.

Somehow it all had changed. The kitten had transformed into an adolescent punk tiger. The group communally swam through the section I remembered as easy which troubled them because I had said the gorge, lower down, *might* be more difficult. Trying to be reassuring, my words instead had an overall insomniac effect on the group. I know, because they kept me up all night making out their *ad hoc* wills.

By comparison to what we had been through, the gorge proved easy; the routes through the two substantial drops had apparently straightened out over the last four years. As a boater I could hardly believe I'd improved that much. So I decided that some mysterious force must have shuffled the boulders around. If my clients had been speaking to me, I think they would have received my comment with skepticism.

Upon reaching the take-out, the group—joyously exuberant to be alive—graciously spared my life, but only on the condition that I vowed never to lead a commercial trip ever, *ever* again. It was a promise I had no problem keeping. However, sometimes I regret they didn't make me swear off boating altogether.

Whether it was a temporary or permanent decision I don't know, but our clients certainly swore off boating for the remainder of the trip. On our last river, the Pukaki, they all stayed with the van and drove the shuttle while Clyde and I ran the river.

Part III: The Final Revenge
(The Landsborough)

It rained and rained and rained,
The average fall was well maintained;
And when the tracks were simply bogs,
It started raining cats and dogs.
After a drought of half an hour,
We had a most refreshing shower;
And then, most curious thing of all,
A gentle rain began to fall.
Next day was one but fairly dry,
Save for one deluge from the sky,
Which wetted the party to the skin,
And then at last—the rain set in.

—anonymous West Coast pioneer

❖   ❖   ❖

Two years later, something salmon-like and self-destructive sent me back once more to the Landsborough. It was to be just a quiet little two-day excursion, with only Carol, my "other significant girlfriend." We had packed for a light and quick descent. This time we entered the valley by plane, kayaks lashed to the wing struts.

While we were flying in, Carol said, "I thought you told me it was mountainous."

"It will be," I assured her, "As soon as these clouds lift."

"And I know you said the river was blue."

"Well, I'm sure it will be blue as soon as it stops being brown."

Never learning my lesson the first—or second time—I return once more to be put at the mercy of the Landsborough.

As we ate dinner that evening, we watched the sun, for a few heroic moments, try plying apart the clouds to leak a few sallow rays into the valley. Then the clouds banged shut and it was the last we were to know of the sun's existence for the ensuing indefinite future.

Next morning, Carol alerted me to an overwhelming fact. "Didn't the rain wake you up last night?"

"What rain?"

"The same rain that's hitting the tent right now."

"How can it be the same rain if it already fell last night?"

"Don't you hear it?"

"No. Drizzle doesn't make noise."

By the time we were in our wetsuits and our boats were loaded, it was drizzling with such conviction that the river had risen a foot.

The water was cold, which seemed to make the hydraulics vicious—ones that also became obscured in the mist settling on the river. Once, after a narrow escape from disappearing eternally in a large, famished hole, Carol said, her voice emerging from somewhere in the fog, "You know, I don't mind the cloud hiding the mountains, but I do object to this cloud hiding the river."

I said, "Well, let's just camp here and wait for better weather tomorrow." Which, with better weather still another seven months off, was something akin to waiting for morning on the dark side of the moon.

To gauge the river's ominous rise, I placed four sticks up the bank over a six-foot span, then we walked into the gorge. Immediately the fog dissipated—but I wished it hadn't, for only then did I realize just how high the river was. If the first drop had been accessible by road, it would have quickly turned into one of New Zealand's major tourist attractions capable of supporting a small town the size of Auckland. Gigantic, roiling waves leapt and sloshed and collapsed exactly the way they used to in my parent's bathtub when I staged the World's Greatest Sea Battles. Boulders clinked and rumbled down the bed. Eddies were nothing but boat-swallowing whirlpools.

"Geez," Carol said with the tone of someone partaking in a natural disaster, "I had no idea the river was *this* hard."

Of course, modesty prevented me from admitting that my previous encounters with the river concerned about one one-thousandth of this present volume. Portage was feasible, but with the river rising there was no guarantee of escape from the four or so miles of gorge beyond. And yet, there was something else about the river that bothered me. Twenty or so feet above the present water level, the banks and rock were bare. If the river was presently in flood, *why the heck was that scrubbed clean?*

Returning to camp I checked my gauge sticks. In just two hours the river was now working on the fourth stick. But I merely shrugged and said, "Well if it can rise with such business-like effort it can damn well drop just as fast." Feeling like Noah, I looked up. All it had to do was stop raining. Then another sandfly bit me and I didn't feel like Noah any more, and instead I cursed the old fool for being so pedantic about his two-animal commitment.

Our remaining food inventory amounted to one dinner, one lunch, one breakfast, instant soups, and a quarter pound of coffee. These meals we would save until the river dropped to a runnable level and our energy would be required. This left a menu a cretin could plan: breakfast—coffee; lunch—hot water; dinner—soup. Yet realizing the inadequacy of this menu we quickly changed it to: *café, chaud eau,* and *potage du Lipton.*

Staying dry meant only wearing our clothes in the tent; outside, we wore our paddling gear. For fire-starts we had plenty of matches, two lighters, and a small flank of inner-tube rubber. The only wood available was silver beech, a fuel so miserable that insurance companies should demand that houses be built from it.

Heating water proved a major chore. The vast quantities of smoke didn't deter the sandflies either; in fact, they appeared to prefer smoked meat.

Captain Cook wrote:

"The most mischievous animal here is the small black sandfly which are exceedingly numerous and are so troublesome that they exceed everything of the kind I have ever met with,[4] wherever they light they cause a swelling and such an intolerable itching that it is not possible to refrain from scratching and the last ends in ulcers like the smallpox."

Appropriately, his next sentence reads:

"The almost continual rain may be reckoned another inconveniency attending this Bay [Dusky] but perhaps this may happen at some seasons of the year, yet the situation of the Country, vast height and nearness of the Mountains seem to subject it to much rain at all times."

So, with the weather suitable for building an ark or for soothsaying doom, Carol and I settled in. We spent the day finishing our books, then switched, but I was tired of reading.

"I hate waiting," I complained.

"And what would you be doing that's useful right now?" Carol inquired.

"Procrastinating."

On the second day, bored with reading, I caught up on tasks that really, *really* needed to be done—ones that I had always before put off. For example, I began picking at my feet. After an hour or so, thoroughly pleased with the effort, I took to cleaning my Swiss Army knife, which reminded me of a story about a friend, a person sentimentally attached to his Swiss Army knife beyond all money and reason. He owned an old knife—one of the first—given to him by his father, and the blade was worn down to nothing but a memory. But the knife was dirty, a problem easily overcome, his girlfriend assured him, by dropping it in boiling water—which he did. To his horror the red plastic immediately peeled away from the knife body and turned into something alive, writhing in pain as if scalded; then it shrank and died, twisted like rotini. "Huh! Isn't

---

[4] Written before he met the Hawaiians.

that something!" his girlfriend exclaimed incredulously. "Mine did the exact *same* thing!"

On the third day, after finishing our books and not wanting to start rereading, we reduced them to a deck of cards. Unfortunately, it didn't take more than one game of rummy before we each accused the other of memorizing page numbers.

The following day, after several giant helpings of *chaud eau*, a bigger disagreement began. It started with Carol brushing her teeth for the second time that day.

I said, "Look—hot water does not cause cavities."

She shrugged and continued her brushing, irritating me even further. Then she stopped brushing and put her toothbrush away. I waited for her to spit. But nothing happened. I waited some more—but still nothing. At last I asked, "Aren't you going to spit that out?"

"I swallowed it."

"You *swallowed* it?"

"Sure, I got hungry."

"So that's why you've been brushing your teeth! You've been eating toothpaste!"

The ensuing argument spun in circles. I accused her of sneaking an extra snack; she claimed fewer cavities.

Finally, she thrust the tube in my face and said, "Go on, eat your fill!"

I stared at it and finally admitted I wasn't that hungry. For the rest of the day we said about three sentences to each other. Not that we were no longer mad, it was just that we'd covered every subject in the universe at least six times. Staring for days at a soaking, jaundiced tent wall atrophies the imagination. At last I said, "If a spaceship came down right now would you leave on it?"

"It depends," she answered hesitantly.

"Nope," I said. "Can't depend on anything. You'd just have to take your chances."

"There've got to be conditions."

"Nope."

"Then I won't go," she said decidedly.

"OK, OK, what if there are no Young Republicans and there's superior sex and they serve all the gourmet food you can eat and you won't get fat?"

"I doubt it. What if they were here just to conduct a scientific

Carol, day four, shortly
after clandestinely
consuming all available
sources of toothpaste.

experiment and feed you nothing but McDonald's hamburgers all day and make you listen to idiot talk show hosts to see which comes first, McCancer or Insanity?

"They'd never do that."

"Oh yes they would."

"Would not."

"You have a sick mind."

"Only a sick mind would think of *foie grasing* someone with hamburgers while subjecting them to talk show radio with no off switch."

"And what if they played nothing but narrative country songs about dysfunctional kayak trips?"

"That's deranged."

"You're deranged. You brought up this conversation."

"Don't talk to me."

"Don't talk to me, either!"

It wasn't until morning that we did talk, excited by waking up to the sound of rain *not* falling on the tent. Immediately we got up, built a fire, and cooked the remaining dinner. In the meantime we packed. But when it came time to eat we were so anxious that, despite living on nothing but coffee and soup for the last four-and-a-half days, we couldn't swallow a bite.

By the time we were on the river it was raining once more. It took us all day to get through the gorge, and on one long portage, after carrying our gear downstream, we were nearly cut off from our boats by the rising water. Rain, of course, escorted us right to the end.

The next day we drove quickly north for a drier climate, and over the following week we monitored the West Coast weather. Nonstop rain. Then it happened: a wholesale twenty-five-inches-in-twenty-four-hours dump drenched the region. In an instant, all my Landsborough questions were answered. I knew how the rapids came to be re-sculptured between my first and second runs, and I knew why, when the river already seemed to be in flood, there was still a high-water mark several fathoms above me. I have no idea what percentage of the world's water supply is carried by rivers but I knew at that moment that the Landsborough was carrying the lion's share. Lying on a sunny beach, slapping the occasional sandfly, I smiled the smile of the smug, glad I wasn't involved in the carnage.

Somewhere in the upper Motu. Although it may appear that bedrock is causing the turbulence, most of the white is actually starved eels churning the waters to get at me. [Carol Haslett photo]

THE MOTU

Dreaming of a Whitewater Christmas

*For three years I had been well accustomed to sit on the floor of
the canoe (never using a cushion or even a mat), and at once to
apprehend the various knocks, and vibrations, and grazings
received, which are quite distinguishable as the boat passes over
rocks, boulders, shingle, gravel, sand, mud, or weeds. This feeling
of the object outside, through the thin oak plank (not an inch from
your body), is almost as easy as by the hand itself, and therefore I
knew in a moment that some hard, smooth, heavy substance was
knocking below against my boat, and moving forward. The most
likely of all things was that this was a crocodile.*

—John MacGregor, *The Rob Roy on the Jordan,* 1870

❖   ❖   ❖

On one of Captain Cook's visits to New Zealand, he dropped off—
much to the crew's delight—a bunch of pigs. Supposedly the pigs
were to help feed ship-wrecked survivors. This made the Maoris extremely
happy, for it offered them a change of menu from the usual, ship-wrecked
survivor. Not only was the pork more tender, but the pigs were also easier
to clean. Yet the arrangement also must have confused the Maoris. What
were they to think of a culture that said, "Well, instead of improving navigation, we'll just drop pigs off all over the world where our ships are going
to crash. . . ." probably the same thing the British would have thought

had the Maoris landed in Great Britain and dropped off canoe-loads of moas.

In the remote regions of the North Island, the pigs still run feral. In theory this seems a sound idea, since these regions also contain some good kayaking and the chances of wrecking or losing a boat are also good. You know, sort of the modern, twentieth-century shipwreck. But any kayak-wrecked survivor who thinks he is going to step into the bush and subsist on bacon is a kayaker with a serious brain malfunction. The pigs that survive come from a genetically enhanced line, a strain that learned to outrun Maoris.

One of the largest natural[1] pig habitats in the country is around the East Cape region, specifically the Motu River. Although the upper reaches of this river are pastoral and sheep-infested—which probably accounts for the river's wonderful murky-green hue—the lower fifty-five-mile section has hills crowding it that are referred to as mountains. Whether these *are* mountains or not, I'm not going to argue. I do know, however, that the Tarzan-oriented vegetation that smothers them would severely hinder an escape from the valley, unless you are adept at swinging on vines.

My escape, though, was to the valley. Carol and I were hiding from Christmas. Now, don't get me wrong about Christmas. There's nothing I like better than the slow pace of a good Christmas traffic jam to bring my fellow man good cheer and, as he fights to buy the last Nintendo, peace on earth. I dread to think what the leading economic indicators would do if we returned to the old standard of sleigh bells ringing instead of cash registers. As a protest, I used to send my Christmas cards out in the middle of summer, an idea I thought original to the point of genius. However, my enthusiasm was totally squashed one day when, I realized that *everyone* in the Southern Hemisphere sends their Christmas cards out in the middle of summer. And, as I subsequently discovered, the temperate climate in New Zealand has totally mutated the holiday season. In an eighty-degree environment, fake snow in the corner of store windows is hardly convincing. Santa in his winter garb looks like the perfect S-and-M perversion. His most famous quote, "Ho, ho, ho," sounds more like the mournful last gasps of a person locked in a sauna.

So on our escape, setting off down the Motu river, we made a pact not even to mention the big C-word. As for the run itself, providing a flood didn't drown us and wash us into the Bay of Plenty

---

[1] As opposed to Auckland.

(plenty of what, no one could say, but I suspect kayak gear) the river promised some classic whitewater. Actually, the river didn't promise this; some boaters who told us to run it did. So did the local guide book.

That book also advised there was virtually no camping for the first seventeen miles as the river went through two gorges. Now, when I think of two gorges I think of one gorge followed by another gorge, with some ungorge-like behavior in between. Not in this upper section. Here space for gorges is at a premium; the two are smunched together so close it takes a geologist with a magnifying glass to detect the difference.

Flooding was also noted, both by the guidebook and myself: A scoured no-man's land rose twenty to thirty feet above the currently non-flooding river. In one recorded instance, the river had, overnight, gone from forty cubic feet a second to *six thousand*. But the guide's most notable item was this little gem, an extra incentive not to miss a roll: *"Motu eels deserve special mention—many as thick as a man's leg and they seem to be exceedingly hungry. It is not advisable to be in the water after dark as they have been known to attack humans at this time."*

The river was just cloudy enough to obscure my view of the life that I knew was lurking within it, feeding my suspicions that only an all-too-thin layer of fiberglass separated my personal rump steak from a river teeming with eels, the bigger ones no doubt inhabiting the pools below nastier rapids.

In short, the price we were paying to escape Christmas was to share a large, flood-prone trench all day with eels giant enough to star in their own Hollywood horror flick. But these were just abstract and potential problems, nothing like the real one that developed as we descended. Due to various uncharted rocks, our boats began leaking. They were only a week old and now, quite literally, we were breaking them in. When ordering the kayaks, I had specified heavy-duty. They were fifty pounds each so the first criterion had been met, but the "duty" was neglected. In a matter of hours the boats were wearing half a roll of duct tape between them. Ironically, we were carrying a dozen raw eggs packed only in their cardboard container and *not one* of them cracked. Pulling ashore to fix another hole, I kicked my boat and immediately had another crack to repair. With four-and-a-half days yet to go on a rapidly diminishing roll of tape, it looked like we might be hunting pigs after all. But it was darkly comforting to know we were not the only people who had suffered such a problem. At the river's hardest drop, "The Slot," we discovered two wrecked kayaks abandoned in the brush; they were the same make, the same pie-crust construction.

We reached camp at dusk, just as the exceedingly hungry leg-sized eels no doubt began prowling the river, cruising for kayakers foolish enough to linger in the water.

The next day the valley temporarily yawned and vegetation, not rock, flanked the river. One such plant was the cabbage tree, a Dr. Suess designer plant. Around forty-feet tall, these trees contained no foliage except for a single cluster at the end of each branch. We also saw the rare, dove-gray Blue Mountain ducks. Crouching along the river's edge as we passed, they apparently believed they were going unnoticed—which is, of course, the reason why they are rare.

After floating a handful of miles we came to a permanent camp and would have passed right by had it not been for a ribbon of smoke advertising someone's presence. We stopped, hoping for some river information.

The camp's lone occupant met us as we stepped from our boats. He said, "I really don't like boaters coming ashore here, I've got cyanide all over the place."

"Cyanide?"

"For trapping possums. It's horrible stuff. They scream when they die."

"That's OK," I said, "We'll shove back off. We were just wondering what you knew about the river."

"It bloody well nearly flooded me out of my own camp."

"You know anything about it downstream?"

"Nothing but bloody waterfalls and whirlpools!"

"You've seen it then?"

"No way! The kayakers told me. I wouldn't go near it. The bloody thing's filled with eels."

"Well, thanks. We'll be going."

"You'd better have a cuppa tea first."

After emptying six cups of tea and supersaturating our kidneys close to failure, Carol and I learned the trapper's name was Beaver. While Carol and I were eluding Christmas, Beaver was eluding most concepts of civilization—like washing. And as much as he espoused the life of a recluse, he sure seemed starved for company.

Every time we finished our tea, Beaver snatched the tea billy from the coals and refilled our cups.

Whenever we asked anything about the outside world or his past, Beaver became vague, as if suffering from mild amnesia. But when we asked him about life in the bush we couldn't shut him up. Like only yesterday, walking his trap line, he'd unknowingly stepped between a wild sow and her piglets. The sow charged. Having only a single shot .22, he had to be certain that his bullet wouldn't stray. He shot the pig at ten feet; it dropped dead at his feet. He said we'd have it for "tea."

"But we've got to be going," I insisted.

"It's only going to go to waste if you don't stay." Then he asked what day it was.

"December twenty-fourth," I said.

"I thought so," he said sadly, but then, in the same breath and a revived eagerness, added, "It'll be our Christmas pork."

I helped him fetch the carcass, which was in a gunny sack, but the flies had got to it anyway and blown all but a shoulder. After carving the good meat off, he asked, "You seen any eels yet?"

"Not yet."

"I'll show you bloody eels!"

We carried the carcass down to the water's edge, Beaver tied a line around a leg, tied the line to the bank, and pushed the remains into the river.

That evening pork hissed in the frying pan. We gorged ourselves then lay back, watching the darkness push the evening pastels from the sky. At last, when the stars were out in full bloom, we checked the carcass. We trooped down to the river's edge and Beaver, holding a kerosene lantern aloft, proclaimed, "That's why I don't go swimming in the bloody river!" I could hardly see the carcass for all the eels dangling from it. I leaped to a boulder for a closer look, not seeing that the boulder was slimy and that a foot would never adhere to it. My momentum carried me into the water, landing me squarely on the carcass. All I was wearing were shorts. All I felt were eels slithering over my body. Jesus might have walked on water, but I ran.

The next morning—each of us carefully avoiding any mention of what day it was—Beaver cooked up more pork. Tea, of course, washed it down, and when our cups were empty we insisted they not be refilled, that we really had to be leaving.

Carol asked Beaver for an address where she could send him a card but he sadly admitted he didn't have one. So we thanked him, wished him luck, and floated away—but not before noticing the pig carcass stripped clean.

We paddled the remaining gorge. It was wider and less technical; with the greater volume there was little worry about adding additional holes to our boats. However, in this section helmets became an essential piece of equipment; as they scrambled for safety, the wild goats on the cliffs were forever showering us with rocks. When we came to the end of the gorge, we camped. That evening, as we ate dinner, clouds crowded across the sky and shortly afterwards it began to sprinkle. We went to bed.

When the drizzle stopped I awoke, immediately becoming aware of a strange twinkling. Looking out the tent screen, I saw the whole valley aglow with dim fairy-like lights. I said, "Carol, wake up."

"Why?"

"Are you awake?"

"No."

"I won't say what day it still is, but look outside."

We stayed awake for the rest of Christmas gazing at hundreds of glow worms clinging to the nooks of the cliffs.

I wish this story ended there, but it doesn't. Several months later while staying with a friend I told him of our trip down the Motu and of the possum trapper we'd stayed with. He said, "You say, possum trapper?"

Then he began to dig through a pile of newspapers until he found the article he wanted me to read. It was about an escaped convict who had been hiding out in the Motu Valley. The police had finally caught up with him.

THE TOUTLE

Life After Death

But if you are going at full speed down a rapid, and suddenly enter a whirlpool, the water does in reality take hold of the bottom of the boat at one end and forcibly drag it to one side, while the general motion being onward, the result will infallibly be an upset, unless you act wisely. The proper thing to do is to stop the speed of the boat as much as possible, and to lean inwards (not outwards as is always a desire to do), just as the acrobat in a circus leans towards the centre more and more, the faster the horse he is riding gallops round the ring. . . .

—John MacGregor, *The Rob Roy on the Baltic*, 1892

◆　◆　◆

The river was gray, the rocks were gray, the banks were gray, the sky was gray, and so was Lance's VW that we sat in as we watched a wind-driven rain pelt the windshield. With the wipers turned off the picture looked like a colorless van Gogh. Awaiting us was a disaster scene where you'd expect to see the local Eyewitness news reporter with one hand on his wind-harassed microphone while the other holds up his hood:

Reporter: "I'm standing here . . . Bob, at the site where a bridge actually used to be before the devastating St. Helen's flood came down this actual river and, as if that bridge had been a mere toy, the flood washed it away! But what's so incredible about this . . . Bob, is it's like this all happened yesterday."

◄ The Toutle, May 18th, 1980—or rather a liquidated Mt. St. Helen's temporarily using the Toutle's bed. [Roger Werth, "The Daily News" photo]

Anchor: "And how long ago was that . . . Al?"

Reporter: "Six months now . . . Bob."

Anchor: "That's very interesting . . . Al. Tell me . . . Al, Wait! Just a minute . . . Al, I think I actually see, yes! There in the background! A car with actual kayaks on it and there seems to be . . . actual live people in that car! Is that right . . . Al?"

Reporter: "Yes, indeed it is . . . Bob."

Anchor: "This is a very interesting new angle . . . Al."

Reporter: "That's right . . . Bob, but the angle you are seeing is because of our cameraman . . . Joe. Joe's left leg . . . Bob, has sunk up to his knee in mud while his right leg has only sunk to his right ankle."

Anchor: "I see. These kayakers . . . Al. They don't actually plan to run this river do they?"

Reporter: "Yes indeed they do . . . Bob. In fact . . . Bob, kayakers used to run this section of river quite frequently, but this is the first known attempt to descend this *incredibly treacherous* section of the Toutle river, since Mt. St. Helen's *devastating* eruption."

Anchor: "And have you actually talked to them . . . Al?"

Reporter: "I have . . . Bob."

Anchor: "And what do they expect to find downriver?"

Reporter: "No one quite knows . . . Bob. As you remember, the entire contents of Camp Baker was washed down into this canyon, and Camp Baker included thousands upon thousands of logs, logging trucks, and . . . an entire railway . . . Bob. There were also twenty-five bridges like the missing one I'm now standing in front of that were also swept away in the flood's rampage. These . . . Bob, could all lie choking off the river downstream, a horrible gnarled twisted mass of wreckage—testimony to just how powerful this mud flood was. And all this . . . Bob, could be dangerously blocking any hope that these kayakers successfully navigate this river today. We could actually be witnessing the last anyone ever sees of these three."

Anchor: "And what are these kayakers doing now . . . Al?"

Reporter: "Bob, they're sitting in their car, where they've been for the last half an hour going over final plans and quite frankly . . . Bob, I believe they are trying to warm themselves up. As you can see . . . Bob, it's near freezing out here and with the rain blowing sideways, it makes for quite a chilly—brrrrr—Thanksgiving day. Just makes us all appreciate warm houses, a nice meal, and a football game, doesn't it . . . Bob?"

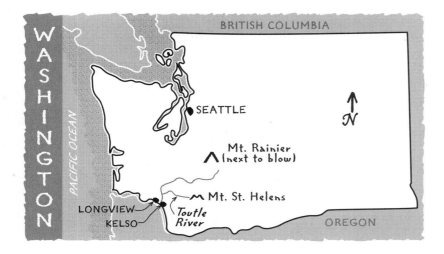

Anchor: "Yes, indeed it does . . . Al. Thank you for that report . . . Al. Al Fresco reporting live from the Toutle."

Anchor (now speaking solely to viewers): "We'll keep you up to date on any further developments on this fascinating story and now a word from our sponsor, Lava soap. . . ."

◆ ◆ ◆

In the beginning, when Mt. St. Helen's erupted, I was on a fishing boat in Alaska. News was sketchy, so the a death toll was solely arrived at by radio rumor. As the day wore on this casualty figure constantly rose until it assumed a new, augmented dimension: Several towns had been erased. Surely this meant Kelso and Longview, Helen's closest targets rendered into modern-day Pompeiis. Buried under acres of ash these towns, instantly entombed *in flagrante delicto*,[1] would be outstanding natural monuments to the advance of civilization since the uncouth Romans.[2] Archaeologists could dig up ash-molded people engaged in modern twentieth-century routines: a bank robbery here, a drug deal there, a teenage pregnancy in the making, a vandal misspelling his graffiti, a city hall filled with corruption and, well—you get the idea.

But, of course, my imagination got carried away. Instead, the eruption burst out the mountain's north side, oozing a 50-m.p.h., 100-degree slurry of hot ash and melted snow down the Toutle drainage, something so simple I didn't even think of it. What then

---

[1] That's Latin.

[2] Who used words like, *in flagrante delicto*.

boggled me was that the press made a really big deal out of it. I mean we're talking about the super-saturated Northwest,[3] a mud-aligned society already. So with my imagination embittered about being humbled by an excessive amount of mud, it immediately started down another tangent. It pondered: Bet that Toutle's one hell of a run right now.

For the Northwest, the Toutle had been unique (not that what Helen's had done to it made it common). Unlike all the other challenging runs that coursed through wilderness-like settings, the lower Toutle was a class 4 section in the middle of a rural region. When I thought that a descent of this remodeled river was a creative idea, I first had to wait until the fall rains put adequate water into it . . . . Now, wading through the mud to put on the Toutle, listening to Lance and Carol complaining, I tried distancing myself, arguing that this outing was not solely my idea.

I said, "If you two hadn't listened to me, *we* wouldn't be here right now."

Both readily agreed. However, neither of them suggested slogging back through the mud and returning the boats to the roof of the car. Instead, Carol, as if resigned to some new and different twist of fate, muttered, "Thanks to your last imaginative plan we all have police records now."

"Yes, but it wasn't my fault we were caught." (Well, actually, it *was* but how was I to know we had picked the opening day of fishing season to sneak onto the Cedar River, which is the source of Seattle's drinking water, and that the watershed guards would all be out in force looking for the inevitable trespassing fisherman? Unknown to us we were spotted immediately, pursued down the entire watershed, and caught within hundred yards of our get-away car. True, there was a long open pool impounded by a nasty weir that required a portage, all of it very much exposed to the watershed's office building. Then there was that cyclone fence . . .)

Lance, placing his boat on the Toutle, said, "You could have at least done our community labor for us."

"Not to mention paying our fines," Carol added.

"Hey, when are you two going to look at the bright side? That fifty bucks could have been a thousand *and* you could still be in jail!"

However, I thought to myself, if I were in jail, at least my hands wouldn't be frozen right now; I could hardly work my spray-deck on. When the current swung my boat around I dipped my

[3] A low-lying region now filled with low-lying people.

paddle into the river. The blade disappeared. Pulling the blade felt more like shoveling dirt than pulling water. The sand in the water vibrated through the shaft. Small waves washed over my deck leaving a layer of sand, which was quickly swept away and replaced by the next splash. Breaking through a set of larger waves I received a sand-blasting; grit blasted my eyes and stuck between my teeth. Not that I am a connoisseur of cement slurry, but the water tasted distinctly of acid. It reminded me of my first kiss in high school—my first bitter taste of lust. We'd just been taught about relative pH and there I was, sucked onto some girl's face, trying to guess her pH, wondering what education would teach me next.

As I grabbed my first eddy my boat spun around, then jarred to a stop. The excessive sediment in the river perpetually filled in the eddies creating a veneer of water—and an enticing facade. Quickly I pushed myself off to watch Carol and Lance repeat my performance, driving, one after the other expecting fast turns—only to jolt to a stop like little Noahs run aground.

The old classic Toutle run was composed of two gorges interpolated by a section of calmer water. In this first canyon, the river was settling back to its old and solid rock bed. Big boulders remained with unmoved familiarity, but little ones had been tossed around like crap dice. As if the gorge was chalk-lined, twenty feet above the present level of the river ran the almost precise tell-tale flood line. The line demarcated life: above, the walls glistened green; below, a frosting of muck. The air was weighted with a raw sweet smell, like freshly bulldozed earth. The rinsing rain loosened hunks of mud which plopped incessantly into the river, broadcasting the unstable conditions—and adding yet more sediment to the water.

Because of the sediment, the river no longer dropped and pooled; there was just big slop and little slop and the gradient was constant. The sediment made reading difficult, for there was no telling what debris lay hidden below the surface, like choker cables or a bridge's rebar or Camp Baker's cutlery. Working carefully downstream—without actually walking—we avoided all irregular and suspicious-looking water. We had no intention of being associated with headlines that read:

Boater dies pinned against radiator of '76 Kenworth truck

I had expected to find massive log jams in this section, but evidently

59

Living on the edge. Most
of the people living along
the Toutle did not have
flood or volcano insurance
and lost everything.
[Al Fresco photo]

the logs had been carried on the flood's crest, keeping them far above the boulders we were presently negotiating.

When at last the first canyon yielded to openness, I reckoned the degree of difficulty would ease, but instead this area offered a host of hazards. The channel became hopelessly lost. Since there were no walls to herd it, the mud flow spread across a half-mile-wide passage. It snapped off stands of new-growth alder and fir leaving acres of jagged stumps. Lying among these were crumpled container cars, pieces of logging trucks, and unidentifiable wreck-age. A massive steel span from a bridge lay draped like a wet egg noodle around a house-sized rock. Several times the current swept us through vast stump fields where fortunately the flow was slow enough to enable us to slalom around these piling-like obstacles.

In this segment, houses and small farms used to flank the banks. Screw up here and you could swim ashore right into some-one's back yard and have your wetsuit removed in hunks by a Rottweiler. The flood also destroyed one-hundred-and-twenty-five houses—not factoring in the doghouses. Many were swept down-stream intact only to have their roofs sheered off (homes, not doghouses) as they smashed into the I-5 bridge—one of the few bridges to survive the flood. But other houses remained. One hung precariously on an undercut bank; the mud had knocked others off their foundations, twisting and cracking and tearing them open. Inside one house sat a half-drunk bottle of wine on a table; we couldn't decide if this was the scene of a hasty escape or if the owner had returned and tried to nurse his sorrow. He might even have been an old Peace Corps worker speculating a thread-bare dictum: Is my house half-full or half-empty of mud? He had plenty to be sorry for. We imagined the scene: The steaming mud, like a sci-fi monster, oozed up the side of the house and shoved in the sliding glass door. Then it ravaged the TV, the fridge, the oven, the couch, and everything else right up to the table's level, where the wine sat. Too bad, we commented, that the wine wasn't hot and spiced. While my teeth chattered in time to the imagined theme song of *The Twilight Zone*, I thought, "funny how the novel idea of running this river seemed great in the comfort of warmth."

Near this scene of misfortune used to be a pre-flood play hole marked by another house. With the house gone, I couldn't even guess where the hole might have been. What we did find to play were sandwaves, something the three of us knew nothing about. In flat spots, for no apparent reason, sets of perfect standing waves suddenly appeared—which we readily jumped on. But no sooner would we do so than the waves simply vanished—leaving us to wonder if they had been there at all.

Finally, thoroughly wet, shaking cold, and remorseful that we weren't masochists so that we could enjoy such bone-numbing moments, we arrived at the second canyon. All day it had continued to rain with an earth-soaking pursuit and we were suddenly aware of the river's quick rise. The first hint of dusk was already bruising the low gray sky. Since our curiosity about the run had already been saturated, all we desired of Thanksgiving was a thermos of coffee and a car heater. Salvation lay at the end of this section where the walls tightened, squeezing into Hollywood Gorge, creating and entertaining the hardest drop on the river. Here, the canyon's bullying had shoved the mud line about twenty-five feet above us. We approached a rapid where the river hurried down a giant rock alley around a blind corner. With the present flume-like velocity we weren't sure if we could stop for any unseen hazard. Pulling out for a scout we walked down a wide shelf where a small stand of fir once shaded the river. The trees measured about six inches in diameter and the mud had bent them all downstream, stripped their branches and sanded them smooth. Our scout revealed no hazards.

Arriving at Hollywood Gorge we eddied out for one last look. The route was a simple tongue followed by a sashay right to miss a giant hole, an appropriate heart-thumping climax for the run—on a good day. But now, freezing, I could care less. After the anticipation of all the river's unknown hazards, there it flowed, still tediously the same. I stared at it, thoroughly annoyed that my imagination had delivered me to this moment. Nothing in the world could beat a sunny day and whitewater. Hollywood Gorge contained neither. Really, I don't know what hidden pleasures I had expected from our run. Yet dashed expectations are all relative. Walking out the lane that led from the Gorge and the wreckage of the Toutle still hung an old and familiar sign that read:

> "Friends, The beauty of this land is within your hands.
> Please do your part to put litter in its place."

I thought: "I wonder who that person was trying to fool?"

Carol shopping for flip-flops on the Tama.

JAPAN

For a Thong

If you stick your elbow out too far, you'll leave it on someone else's car.

—The Burma Shave fracture

◆　◆　◆

I realized I was not suited for Japan when I ordered my first cup of coffee in the Narita airport. I was waiting for George Kosen at the time. I'd already given the waitress roughly half my year's wages, when she said something about change. I said, "yes, where is it?" which is the exact thing she wanted to know. She needed *more* money. I hadn't been on the ground more than a half an hour and it was looking like I'd have to file for bankruptcy if I wanted to finish my coffee.

Going to Japan wasn't my idea at all. It was the brainchild of a) George, who had moved back there and said to come see him, and b) Carol; she said, "OK, we will."—"We," involving me. George was a boater I'd met in the Northwest while paddling a river that went past his yard or, when the river flooded, *through* it. At last, tired of life's complexities in the U.S. and, most of all, tired of kayakers doing endos in his garden, George got up one day and said, "OK that's it, I've had enough of this. I'm moving back to Tokyo!"

Carol, I'd only known then a few months. She said she wanted to see the world.

"Where?" I asked.

"The whole thing," she answered and proceeded to sell off everything she owned to fund such a project.

The next day we bought two Pan Am around-the-world-in-eighty-day tickets. Only later did we realize they meant eighty delays. I'm sure there are still some Pan Am planes out there awaiting parts, unaware that the company no longer exists.

With seventy-eight days to go (the dateline swiped one, and the holding pattern over Narita got another) our first stop was Tokyo. Just as I was wondering where George was, and about to sign a contract to pay for my cup of coffee in monthly installments, George's voice didn't say, "Whit, Carol, where have you been?" Someone else's did.

George, it turned out, wasn't even in Japan. Unexpectedly grounded by an airline strike in the U.S., he had sent his proxy and kayaking buddy, Wayne Jordan, to fetch us. Wayne said not to worry about a thing, which was a lie, because as soon as we were out on the road, I was worried about my well-being. With Wayne, I brushed death more often than I've ever brushed my teeth. Arcade games were nothing but a slow-motion Sunday outing compared to Wayne's idea of car-passing choreography.

Wayne took us to his house where he was entertaining a circus, a European troupe performing in Tokyo. A Swiss said to me, "So you're another kayaker. I sink you're insane. Zat is very dangerous."

"What do you do?" I asked.

"I do acrobatics off a tethered plane zat my wife controls from da ground."

"Isn't *that* dangerous?"

Before he could answer, another circus member leaned into the conversation and said, "Only ven his vife is mad at him."

Over the next week, Wayne took us on various excursions. I can't say I really saw Honshu, let alone Japan's other main islands.[1] Life outside the car passed by in the same blur it did inside. And as Japan went past in large nondescript streaks, Wayne began teaching us important phrases we would eventually need to know, such as: "Beer," "More beer," and, "I promise I won't toss my cookies on your Prime Minister."

We tried these phrases out on various unsuspecting and innocent Japanese and, in turn, they were exceptionally polite, nodding back at us, all the while searching for the nearest fire escape to leap off of. Despite what some (bitter American U.S. car owners) claim, the politeness is only a front; underneath the Japanese hold most foreigners in contempt—unlike, say, the honest and loving attitude with which one is greeted in Miami or New York.

---

[1] Horseshu, AwChu, and Gesundheit.

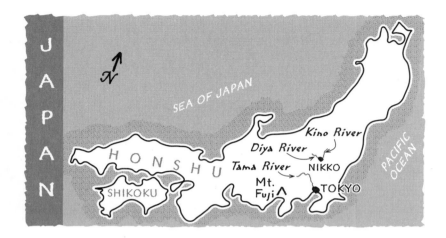

True, a Godzilla alter ego emerges when the Japanese get behind the steering wheel, but even after an accident I can only imagine civility.

Driver 1: "You just clipped my mirror."

Driver 2: "I'm very sorry."

Driver 1: "No, it's my fault, I shouldn't have had it there for you to clip in the first place."

Driver 2: "Oh no, you are quite mistaken, I shouldn't have been there to clip it. Really, it is my fault. If our government would only let us own guns I would point mine at you right now and make you admit I am to blame."

Not like the U.S. . . . .

Driver 1: "You just clipped my mirror."

Driver 2: "Oh YEAH! Well take this! KABLOOIE!"

But the clogged roads weren't all bad, for with traffic crawling at a snail's pace,[2] Wayne had little opportunity to practice his car slalom skills. When we did move, we drove past the Imperial Palace, a hunk of downtown Tokyo real estate estimated at such a premium that its value could supposedly buy California in its entirety. Such over-inflated prices! But how does one tell these people that California isn't even worth trading for a Liechtenstein junkyard?

The most startling cultural difference I noticed, though, was beer. It was being sold out of pop machines on the street.

Carol said, "Can you imagine what would happen in the U.S. if they did that!"

---

[2] How escargots.

"I can tell you," I answered. "I used to have a Coke machine in my dorm room in college that I sold beer out of."

"What happened?"

"I nearly got kicked out of school."

One day we raced north to Nikko, Japan's Vegas. Wayne said there were a couple of unrun rivers in the region, but a girlfriend had something to do with the real decision. Wayne and George had run most of the rivers within a day's drive of Tokyo. They began in 1969 when Wayne had gone to Europe and returned with the most ripped-off boat in the world: a Lettman—which he and George proceeded to copy. With little experience, they began attacking the rivers. Most runs were done without a topo map and with little idea of what lay downstream. Quickly, two classifications developed: hard and no good. Wayne said that if we were lucky (and if I was lucky enough to survive the driving) September usually presented at least one good typhoon, turning the rivers into such torrents that, if the demolition they predicted was even half true, I couldn't wait to book my reservations out of the country.

While having dinner that evening in Nikko, we were approached by a band member who said he was playing in a small and intimate nightclub. Although he said it would be very hard to arrange, he thought he *might* be able to reserve us a table *if* we were interested. Intrigued by such a rare opportunity, along with the chance to observe Japanese culture up close, we told him by all means, to save us a place.

The nightclub was the size of an auditorium—with the acoustical equivalence of one, too. The audience was made up primarily of men but there were a handful of token geishas, their hairdos containing what appeared to be five gallons of polyester resin. I looked around for our buddy and caught a glimpse of him, hidden behind the crowd; his sole purpose in life was to manufacture back-up noise in the corner.

I thought a little saki might complement what we were about to see, but since everyone around us was drinking beer, we ordered the same—which was good because, I wasn't actually sure how saki would wash down the peanuts we were gobbling from the communal bowl on the table. At last the first act commenced: an all-girls band from Taiwan. They sang disco songs, climaxing their act with "Y.M.C.A." (with authentic hand motions) and I thought, "what the heck? At least they're Asian."

We ordered more beers and, as I waited for the grand finale, I mused: "Here I am! Japan! Land of sophisticated and subtle culture." I imagined a soliloquy from a famous Kabuki, spoken while the actor attempted to set a new world record for changing costumes. Or perhaps it would be a haiku slam. But instead a line of Vegas girls trooped out on stage in outfits with malfunctioning fasteners, for all their tops quickly fell off. Audience reaction was a xerox copy of cub scouts, like the time when I was sent on a scavenger mission, and my buddies and I stumbled across the Den Mother's husband's collection of *Playboys*. I'd never heard such a stunned silence in my life and here it was again . . . . Which wasn't half as stunned as our reaction when we got the bill: one-hundred-and-eight dollars for six beers—and the bill didn't even come with fortune cookies! Wayne, swearing something was wrong, had the bill itemized. But just to show how easily international misunderstandings can erupt, we had indeed jumped to unnecessary conclusions. The beer actually was not one-hundred-and-eight dollars, but a mere *eighty*. The peanuts were *twenty-eight*.

The next morning, half an hour from Nikko, we put in on the Diya. Having deeply researched it from our occasional glimpse out the window while driving up, we started our descent. It was a small river. Behind us, mountains jutted straight up, the drainage a direct, but not a well-developed, product of them. The few structures along the river were mostly hidden by dark green trees and brush. For kayaking the gradient was steep and constant but its low volume lacked power, making the eddies dull. And when at last we did come to a small jet flanked with some snappy eddies, there was a fisherman. As we dropped down the chute he immediately motioned us to leave.

"Ignore him," Wayne said, then added, "I'll talk to him."

As Wayne approached, the fisherman's voice ascended with increased agitation.

"What did he say?" I asked as we left.

"Says, since he has to have a license to fish we shouldn't be allowed to use the river."

"What did you say?"

"I told him we had one."

"And that upset him?"

"No, I told him *he* shouldn't be allowed to use it."

This approach varied diametrically from the one I'd seen

Carol on a Diya.

George use in the States. A fisherman, pulling out a pistol on us, told us in so many colorful words to get off the river. George, paddling up to him, advised him that if he didn't put his gun away, he, George, *would* and that it would require a team of expert proctologists to retrieve it.

When the Diya flattened at last, Wayne's girlfriend fetched us. Having knocked off one unrun river we should have rested on our success. But we drove—wetsuits soaking the seats—to the Kino—and as soon as we put onto it, we knew why it was unrun.

The Kino's gorge was truly unique. It ran through the middle of Nikko, its rock walls doubled in height by the hotels built on top of them. The river, through this unnatural gorge, was small and insignificant until, halfway down, a pipe added mass volume to it. Now the Japanese, although they don't cook their fish, like to cook *themselves* by taking hot baths. If I guessed correctly, this was millions of gallons of abandoned bath water. The grey hue it added to the water made the river completely unlike the spring-fresh Diya. Splashes were not splashes, they were glugs. But at least—unlike the Diya—it also made the river pleasantly warm. So I can't complain about getting hypothermic after dumping in a boulder spill, breaking my paddle, being forced to swim, and swallowing entire eddies of river. Dejected, Carol gave me words of encouragement, "Look," she said, "if you die of some new-letter hepatitis, there's a bright side!"

"What's that?"

"You won't need to be embalmed."

◆   ◆   ◆

In time, George arrived. We set off to see more of Tokyo and decided to do so via subway, which George thought was a good idea until we made our first transfer—and George said it wasn't a good idea after all.

"Why's that?" I asked.

"It's all color coded."

"So?"

"I'm color-blind. We just got on the wrong train."

It was hours before we saw daylight again. Not that George can't speak Japanese. He can, along with Estonian and English and German; when encouraged by alcohol, he can even carry on a simultaneous filibuster in all four languages. But no tongue is adequate for addressing an onrushing Tokyo subway crowd. No sooner would he say, "Excuse me," to a person running past than five hundred more people would pinball off of us and compress into an arriving train. Its doors would slam shut and off it would go, leaving us alone, still lost, and no wiser.

Later in the week (when at last we emerged from the subway), we "climbed" Fuji. Although it inches up toward 12,400 feet, I am certain that if anyone ever decides to recycle the pop cans on top of it, its height will be substantially reduced. It took us four hours to walk up and fifteen minutes to run down.

The next day, George drove us to his and Wayne's cabin along the Tama, a river just outside of Tokyo. George, who had to work, left us with his van, along with our own self-destructive urges. What he failed to tell us, however, was that the river in front of the cabin was owned by a fish stocker who charged people to fish there. The last thing he wanted was kayaks on *his* river. As soon as we put on, the man scrambled down the bank and stood over Carol like a malfunctioning semaphore, thrusting his arms skyward, thrusting his arms earthward, intermittently pointing an accusing finger at the both of us, all the while carrying on with words I was better off not understanding.

I said to Carol, "Obviously, he's assuming we're friends of Wayne and George."

"Then he probably has every reason in the world to be upset."

We retreated, carried the boats several hundred feet downstream, slipped unseen behind a boulder, and once more got into our boats.

Although there were no fishermen on the owned section of river, there were numerous fishermen downstream freeloading off the fish stocker's labor. Plentiful as boulders, they created a slalom between lines. Occasionally, where the river braided, the fishermen would stand mid-river, facing downstream, often in the only navigable spot. With the noise of the rapids, these fishermen never heard us coming. This problem was compounded because neither of us knew Japanese to warn them and we didn't want to yell, confirming any beliefs they might have about loud-mouthed Westerners.[3] So we silently drifted upon them, scaring the daylights out of them. Poor souls: Their one little hunk of tranquility in such a crowded country—and we arrived to mow them over.

[3] And uneducated. The average Japanese third grader knows more than five Harvard graduates.

For being so close to Tokyo the Tama was a pretty little river. Scattered along the banks where clusters of houses, not the two-by-four and plywood species, but delicate-walled houses with red and purple tiled roofs sloping up at the corners to rid the dwellings of evil spirits (like kayakers who scare fishermen). They were small, packed together (the houses, not the evil spirits), and well maintained, yet each differed. When a house didn't line the river, a cliff or railroad or road did. Even here, an endless procession of cars packed the roads. Above the congestion rose steep hillsides covered with broccoli-green trees that contrasted sharply with a smog-dulled, turquoise sky. The valley broadened and soon we ran out of rapids.

Instead of setting up our shuttle ahead of time—running George's van down and taking the train back upstream—we figured we'd fetch the van later, which was easy to say at the time. We quickly regretted our decision. Unfortunately, we hadn't a clue what the word for "train" was and we soon learned that locating a station can be an all-evening project. Our search culminated in a corner grocery where Carol and I tried every conceivable word we knew associated with trains, trying to make the grocer comprehend. The more we tried the more the grocer's face twisted into a knot of confusion until Carol, at last, reverted to extreme basics. "Chu chu chu? You know?"

The grocer's face unwound in an "Oh! I know" smile and with a series of hand gestures indicating a right turn and a left, then go straight and you can't miss it, directed Carol straight to the chewing gum.

The next day we drove back across Tokyo. Not wanting to face rush hour, we figured the traffic might thin by, say, 1 a.m. Unfortunately, as we quickly discovered, the day's first hours belong solely to the trucks, which ply roads hardly wide enough for cars. Occasionally, we'd pass a road sign and Carol would say, "What do you think that one says?"

"Beware of tangled barb wire."

"How about that one?"

"Slippery when earthworms orgy in road."

"And that?"

"Approaching Top Ramen noodles."

As far as oriental Rorschach tests were concerned these signs were invaluable, but for navigational purposes they were useless.

◀ Carol on the Tama. The sign either says, "You are here" or "You shouldn't be here."

Carol, George, and the
Tokyo Canoe Club.

Instead, Carol proceeded to give me readings from her compass. Five hours later we successfully dead-reckoned ourselves across Tokyo.

On the weekend we returned to the Tama with George and put in on the river with the Tokyo Canoe Club. Since it is an individual's sport, kayaking is not a popular activity. Although there are river-running outings, the emphasis is on slalom. Yet the people in the Tokyo Club were as diverse and dynamic as boaters anywhere in the world. Among them was a kite builder, an opera singer (who sang in Italian) and a Buddhist monk who drove a Mercedes. But if they were different in any way it was in their lack of base jokes. I figured that all boaters possess by constitution the lowest order of humor known; I, at least, thought these boaters would be well weathered against such sinister behavior with George and Wayne in the neighborhood, but I was mistaken. At one point George temporarily left his boat and I slipped a rotten fish into it. Several drops later George, discovering his cargo, accused Carol and tipped her over, forcing her out of her boat; then he attacked me. Soon all three of us were swimming and merrily trying to drown each other. Our equipment floated helter-skelter down the river while the club members pretended this was not really happening. They mustered weak smiles that said, "I think I'm going to take up bowling."

In the early evening the three of us returned to the cabin. George left to get some Japanese take-out dishes, but he wasn't gone long since everything he returned with was prepared raw. When we were through stuffing ourselves to the point of exploding and there was nothing left other than a few unreleased burps, one of the Tokyo Canoe Club members showed up at the door. When he left George groaned and said, "We're in trouble."

"How come?"

"Despite your barbaric and immature behavior today, they have just asked us to dinner."

Our reception upon entering the clubhouse resembled a surprise party. They had prepared a meal for us with an uncountable number of courses. George leaned over to me, and in an embarrassed tone, whispered, "You know? Sometimes I wonder if life in the States wasn't easier after all?"

PRIVATE
PURTZ'S
ACCOUNT

The Real Truth

On the worst rapid the "Emma Dean" was swamped and instantly capsized, two fine rifles being lost, along with some bedding. We broke many oars and most of the Ten Commandments. Major Powell said he lost three hundred dollars in bills. I lost my temper and at least a year's growth—didn't have anything else to lose.

—Jack Summer's Account, Robert Brewster Stanton Colorado River Controversies, 1932

❖   ❖   ❖

One day, off hiking by myself in the Grand Canyon, I uncovered a small journal that had been tucked away under a rock. It belonged to one Private Purtz who claimed to be a member of Major Powell's first expedition. I suppose I made a mistake by not showing my find to anyone, for it is gone now. The diary was so fragile that as I went through it and copied its contents, it crumbled to dust. It took me several months to piece together what it said. Not only had the weather taken its toll, but the ants had also eaten up all the punctuation. I took the liberty of reinserting the punctuation, but I have left the entries unedited and the spelling as is.

Private Purtz's Account

i rites this 2 put the record strate. i wuz on major Powell's trip down the Colorado but he seems 2 have 4got the fakt. i have red the major's akount an he got most of it rite. Sum of it wuz stretched an sum wuz jus plane left out. i ain't goin so fur az 2 call the major a liar but like i say i feel the record needs stratening up a grate bit. However its been 25 years now since i run the river an sum of the small 2do's have jus plum e vaporated outa my head. What though i'm tellin about happened cuz i say so an thats the truth.

Furst off, the major makes no menshun of shuttle. i dun that an it wuz no small undertakin. Took me the whole fall, winter an spring of 68 an 9 2 run the wagon down 2 Mohave an ride my horse back. i warnt back more than 2 weeks when we headed off down the river. That wuz summertime. Basically it wuz a good groop however the major did make the mistake of bringin along hiz brother, the captain. The captain wuz an alright creture under normal cercumstance but ours warnt normal an the captain warnt anymore good 2 have along than an old porkypine. The captain always liked a good prank—jus so long as he wuz at the given end. 1 nite he slipt a rattler in2 Dunn's sleeping bag an the captain thot that the funnyist thing, that iz until he burnt down the Howland brothers tent an that wuz even funnier. Course there wuz a good deal of complainin 2 the major bout hiz brother's aktivities but the major told us all not 2 worry. He sez, jus make sure u dont go gittin my brother angry!

The other problem with the captain wuz that when he wuz a kid he'd run sum Road Island crick on a log raft an the major thot that that x-perience wood do r trip sum good. Well it didn't. Strate off the bat the captain crowned hiz self an expert an by an by he b gun sayin how all the rapids on the Colorado wuz nuthin but a piddle compared with what he'd run az a kid. So after every rapid the captain wood tell us how we run it rong. Course he'd never tell us where we wuz spose 2 go b4 the rapids. Why he'd mess up jus az bad az the rest of the boats an we'd call him on it 2 but he'd jus say he had did what he'd dun on purpose.

Az the major said in hiz book r first big hullabaloo came at D saster falls but the major never told how it really happened. i wuz in the *No Name* at the time an we'd jus got in a water fite with *Made of the Canyon*. Well jus 4 a laff 1 of the Howland boys shoved

me overbored an when i tried gittin back in the dam boat tipped
rite over. Corse none of us new D saster falls wuz cumin up an the
No Name wint thru it upside down an that finished her off.
Sumhow the major rekoned it all my falt even though *Made of the
Canyon* started the fite. The major never 4gave me 4 it. That n
cident started bad goin 2 werse. We lost a good deal of r grub an
blongins in the *No Name* but the werse thing lost wuz the silverware.

Not much of nuthin happened fur awhile. The river jus
dragged on an on—sumtimes strate, sumtimes it jus wint in big circles. The major kept on sayin how magnifecent it all wuz, an it wuz
2, cept that sumtimes i got the feeling we wuz jus bugs b in warshed
down a gutter with not much say in the matter. June an July slipt
harmlessly by, r trip goin about az good az a trip can go with nuthin
4 grub but beans, wormy flour, dried apples an coffee an the occasional fried-up rattler. Then in the b ginnin of August the e vent
that made me rite this here akount in the furst place happened.
The major makes no menshun of it in hiz book cents no 1 wooda b
leaved him noways. Hiz credibility wooda shrunk down smaller
than the short end of nuthin. But the followin did happen, cuz i
saw it with my own 2 blu eyes.

Az i said it wuz the b ginnin of august. What day i don't ritely
recall az they wuz all gittin 2 seem about the same. We pulled in2
camp, there, sumwares above lees ferry. The major sez he wuz goin
off scoutin 2 see what wuz downriver an he invites me along. Well
we didn't git far when the major spies a shack, no ordnary shack
but 1 that looks like a biscut 10. My endstinks told me all long we
shooda left well enuf az iz but the major n sisted on touchin it.
Well he wint an touched it sure nuf but no that warnt good enuf
neither an he had 2 go an open the door. Why openin that door
wuz sendin disasster an n vitashun 4 no sooner the door swings
open an a voice sez, "may i help u?"

i looks 4 the owner of that voice an at furst i rekoned my blu
eyes were havin considerble truble adjustin 2 the lite, but really it
wuz *what* they wuz lookin at or ruther *who* they wuz lookin at. They
wuz 2 human beans with faces all polished like apples an not a
wisker on em. Fur clothes they had on a material that looked like
green stovepipes all stuck 2 gether. 1 of em had on the dumbest hat
i ever saw. i wuz stumblin 4 wurds jus a makin baby noises tryin 2
answer but the major he pipes rite up; "i'm major powell the furst 2
run the grand canyon!"

"i see," sez the dumb hat, "u have yer permit?"

"Permit?" sez the major.

"Yes. What did u say yer name wuz?"

"Powell. John Wesley."

"Jus a moment," sez the hatless 1, "i'll check what the computer sez."

"The what?" sez the major.

But the 2 stovepipes ignored him an the hatless 1 runs hiz finger down what musta been what they wuz callen a computor but it jus looked like a plane old paper 2 me. The creture sez, "P . . . Petersen . . . . Nope, don't see yer name here."

Then the dumb hat pipes up. He sez, "U do have a permit mister . . . ."

"Powell, John Wesley, an no i never said no such thing. U see I'm the first 2 run this here grand canyon an . . . ."

"Yes," n terupted the hat. "Many who cum here 2 run the canyon it *iz* there furst time. U'd b surprized how many do cum here who are unaware of r permit sistem."

"Well," sez the major boiling with deplomacy, "Guess u'd bettered give me . . . oh . . . say . . . give me half a dozen of em."

"No, no, i'm sorry jus 1 iz all we allow at a time, jus fill out this form here an i'll point out a few of the regulatshuns we're sort of sticky on."

Well, the major took them forms an started fillin em out with vengence, an wile he duz that the hat b gun a-readin regulatshuns. Why there wuz big regulatshuns, small 1's, blu 1's, red 1's but most of em jus plum didn't make cents. The major he jus ignored the hat until the hat finaly sez, "Now yer aware that yer party must all have p.f.d's?"

The major looked up 2 see if the hat had hiz head screwed on rite. "i tell u pard, most a my party never made it pass the 6th grade. Why Purtz over there didn't even make it past 2nd, did ya Purtz?"

"No sir!"

"Well," sez the hat a great bit muddled, "Rules iz rules an we x pekt u 2 have them."

The major he jus shrugged an went on fillen out papers. Sumtimes the major'd jus about finish but jus then the other 1 goes an gits 2 more fistfulls of papers an throws them down at the major. The major attaks these with even more d terminatshun. The major played rite long, tho, an i think he new az well as i that this wuz no difrent than b in captured by the confederates. They wuz tryin 2 confuze us an make us say things we didn't mean, an let me tell u that hat started throwin sum really big renches in r gears. He sez, "u also reelize u'll have 2 carry all yer fecal matter out."

i didn't no what fecal matters wuz but the major, he wuz up on fecal matters an this upset him. "U want us 2 do what?" sez he.

"Sorry but its the rules. An i mite az well ad that u rn't aloud any fires in the summer either."

"Well then! Jus how u x pect a man 2 cook?"

"Carry a stove."

This disordered the major's mind a great deal an i could tell he warnt fur long on an even keel. "An do u no jus how mucha stove weighs?" the major sez clenchin hiz teeth.

"O, they're really quite nothing!" sez the hat.

"Now listen here pard . . . ." The major stormed, but got cut off at the pass.

"Mister, we didn't make these rules, they . . . ."

"Never mind! Here's yer blasted forms back!"

The hat gave the permit a glance over an announced, "Mister Powell, u've left the preference of dates here blank. Jus when do u wish 2 make yer trip?"

"2 morrow, gall darn ya!"

"O! i'm sorry but that will b quite m possible. There'll b at least a ten year wait furst."

By now u could see lava flowin in the major's eyes. He grasped 4 hiz last breath of sanity an sez, "Pard, ya keep raisin the pot here but ya won't tell me what the game iz. Fun iz fun but this little jokes gone 2 far all ready. i cum here peaceful-like wantin nuthin more from u than a few provishuns 2 help me make my voyage, provishuns that i'll even trade tobacco 4. An n stead u have led me in circles, telling me that my party all must b kollege edukated, then next thing u want them all 2 shit in buckets an carry it down the river, carry it down along with sum 500lb stove which u say iz nuthin at all. Az if i could jump off a cliff an fly an on top that u tell me i can't go down the river 4 a nuther ten years! I have a good noshun 2 blow up yer little shack here."

"OK! OK! OK!" sez the hat all d fensive like. u can go 2 morrow."

"i can?" then why in tar natshun didn't u say so in the furst place?"

"B cuzz we have a nuther sistem here that obveusly u r un aware of that u didn't give me time 2 x plane. u can go commershally."

"How do u mean, commershally?"

"Well, just that. U pay 2 have a rafter take u down."

"Can i still call it my trip?"

"i wood doubt it. Rafters are pretty grudging that way."

"Hmmmm. How much wood this cost?"

"O. U could git a trip 4 a round 1200 dollars."

"1200 bucks! 4 that i damn well oughta b able 2 call it my trip!"

"Mayb but u'll have 2 talk 2 them."

The major just kept shakin hiz head, mutterin, "1200 bucks! 1200 bucks!"

"Yes but 4 that u git food an tents an a guide."

"What's the guide no?"

"Not much, but they can sure fabricate a good yarn."

"What about boats?"

"They're included."

"Can i sell them back at the end of the trip?"

"No, no. They're urs jus 2 ride in 4 the durashun of the trip."

"U mean 4 all that money i don't git 2 keep the boats?"

"No sir."

With this the major b gan 2 really shake hiz head an i wuz gittin 2 worryin it mite not stop.

The hat continued. "Really, u think about that an 1200 dollars per person izn't that bad in this day an age."

"What! U mean 2 tell me that 1200 bucks ain't 4 the hole lot of us!"

"No sir. That's per person."

Well that dun it sure enuf. A bolt of lightening wuz jus molasses compared 2 how fast the major's fist contacted the hat's jaw. Corse hatless didn't take this sittin down an he wuz on the major rite quick but i wuz on him an it didn't take long 4 r 3 arms 2 lick there 4. Only truble wuz we soon found out they wuzn't the only 2 of them critters that lived in them parts an soon the hole lot of em wuz after us like a pack of hounds. We managed 2 ditch em, though, an hi tailed it back 2 camp. It wuz dark by this time an the rest of the group had stoked up the fire thinkin we wuz lost an needed a b con. The furst thing the major sez, all puffin an pantin iz, "Quick boys, douse the fire!"

"What iz it?" askt Sumner.

"Rangers!"

"Ranger injuns?" sez Hall.

"Never herd of em," sez Dunn.

"They ain't injuns boys. They wuz wurser'n that."

"Iz they rusllers?"

"They ain't them neither."

Then 1 of the Howlands pipes up, "Say! this iz an e mergency!" an with that there wuz a mad dash 4 the wiskey an it got drunk up rite quick.

"Iz we gonna fite em or run?" askt Hall.

"Neither," sez the major. "We iz goin down river."

"But major!" Sumner protested, "It's black az chimneys out thare an we git r selfs a hole heep of truble even when its lite! We can't go out thare!"

"Got 2. It's r only hope."

So we packed up an shuved off. Out on the river it wuz that black that the whitewater couldn't b seen. Not 2 say there warnt none cuz there wuz an it soaked us rite thru 2 the teakettles. We were all cold an scared that bad that i could hear sum 1's teeth rat-tlin in the next boat over. Sum 1 said "shut up," an the major told whoever said 2 shut up 2 shut up. We went way pass sunup an lees ferry an finally hauled out in a grotto ware the major reckoned we'd b safe. Still he didn't allow no fires.

After r git away we wuz reel cautious about them rangers but we didn't have no more truble. Bsides, r worrys wuz changin, fur them rapids started gittin bigger. We did notice sumthing strange, 2, bout them that we never did figure out. When we'd git out 2 scout, every drop had a strange smell like ammonia 2 it. We noticed 2 that the bigger the drop the werser the smell.

1 way an another we did git thru that canyon an it wuz a good thing cuz we wuz ready 2 git out. Not on a kounts of the river but the major's brother. He had r nerves rubbed raw. 1 morning we thot he'd reformed cuz he fixed us all oat meal (that wuz r name 4 the wormy flour in boilin water). He'd never cooked at all up till now but here he gone an dun it. Not only did we have oat meal but he'd gone an put raisins in it. Said he'd been a savin them jus 4 a special treat. Well marchin mercurys! We a lit in2 that oatmeal with gusto only 2 d scover it warnt raisins afterall. The darn fool had gone an stuck pollywogs in it. Why the captain thot that even funnier than the Howlands tent burnin down. We didn't, though, an all agreed 2 hang him but hiz brother saved him an suggested that cuz we wuz

so near the end we outa have a little celebrashun an told the Howlands an Dunn 2 hike out an git us sum more hooch. Well, them 3 agreed an set off. Jus a bit later i reckoned i wanted 2 go 2 so i set off after em but i never did catch up with them an its a good thing 2. Sum sez the injuns got em but i aint so sure. I think it wuz them rangers. Anyhow i got lost cumin back 2 camp an when i reached it the major an the rest a the boys had gone, which left me un a kounted 4—which iz how the major never came 2 mentshun me in hiz book.

The lone, surviving picture of Private Purtz. [Royce Ward photo]

One of the greatest joys of paddling in the Himalayas is the solitude.

NEPAL

Surviving a Fall in the Himalayas

Hansen practiced kayak-paddling this afternoon on the pool around the ship, from which several channels diverge over the ice, but he was not content with paddling round in them, but must, of course, make an experiment in capsizing and recovering himself as the Eskimos do. It ended by his not coming up again, losing his paddle, remaining head downwards in the water, and beating about with his hands till the 'kayak' filled, and he got a cold bath from top to toe. Nordahl, who was standing by on the ice to help him, at last found it necessary to go in after him and raise him up on an even keel again, to the great amusement of us others.

—Fridtjof Nansen, *Farthest North*, 1898

◆　◆　◆

Shortly after meeting Dave Manby in Vancouver, I mentioned I was heading off in several day's time to boat in New Zealand. He said, "I've got this friend, Green Slime. You should look out for him."

"Is he going to New Zealand?" I asked, logically enough.

"No," Dave said. "But you never know where you might run into him."

I thought: "Now here's a guy who knows a lot about pigs flying."

Three years passed. Carol and I headed for Asia.

One day we entered a sleazy little bar in Lhasa; it was a joint with a grease-hardened dirt floor, and droves of flies were lazing contentedly about the walls. The conversation was about as lively as the flies; some fool tried to enliven it by talking about a dead person, and quickly a competition emerged over who could tell the most politically correct, morbid story. After a few of these, an American girl with a mouth as big as a six-lane freeway, bragged about gate-crashing a sky burial. She wanted everyone in the bar to be as excited as she was about witnessing bodies sliced and diced and tossed to the vultures like popcorn to pigeons.

Fortunately another storyteller cut her off and, while eagerly rubbing his hands together, he began his tale in an English accent:

"We were, ah, running the Trisuli in Nepal, you see. There were some rafts and some kayaks and, um, we had these Australian girls along. On the last day, one of the girls wanted a go in the kayaks. She'd never been in a kayak before but, um, we let her have a go at it. Well, off she went. She stayed upright until she got to the first rapid then she, um, had a bit of *difficulty* you see. She went for a swim. She tried swimming to shore but got caught in an eddy, you know, one of those things that go round and round behind a big rock. We were a bit of a ways back and saw a vulture circling above her and she was screaming and waving. We thought this was good for a laugh, you know: a hungry vulture, who, um, wasn't going to wait. But as we came closer, we saw why she was really screaming. There was a body in the eddy following her. The more she tried getting away from it, the more it chased her. It, um, wasn't a very *nice* body either. It had only one arm and one leg and the vultures had chewed off its face!"

There were howls of disgust. I waited for the story's end until it became apparent that the story *had* ended, that this grotesque corpse would chase the poor girl for eternity. The teller rubbed his hands even more enthusiastically under the table, obviously pleased with the story's effect.

Carol asked, "What did you do?"

"We put extra iodine in the drinking water that afternoon!"

Overall, the story's effect was like a bucket of slops being emptied on the table. Big Mouth led the exodus out the door until only Carol, the teller, and I were left.

I accused the teller of being English and he confessed he was. I said, "Any chance you know Dave Manby?"

He said, "That's not something a person readily admits, but yes."

"What's your name?"

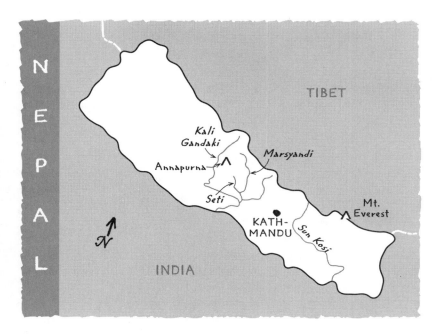

"Green Slime."

"How do you do! I'm Whit Deschner. I've been looking all over the world for you!"

Carol, Slime and I left Lhasa and traveled to Kathmandu together. The contrast between Tibet and Nepal was like dark and light; however, crossing the border at dawn may have had something to do with my impression. Soon afterwards, Slime had to get home, but before leaving he introduced me to Don Weeden.

Although I'd met a Don Weeden six years before on the Rogue River in Oregon, that particular Don didn't have spiked grey hair.

"Believe me," Don said, "This one doesn't either. Not until I was struck by an unnatural phenomena. I looked exactly like the other one until I entered an altered state in Bangkok. This is how I awoke."

Don was an expert on Nepal's rivers. For a college dissertation he had disappeared to Nepal to study the effects of tourism on the Sherpas. However, as his professors later noted, much of his research was conducted from a kayak. This time, Don was back as a population control expert—with his kayak—and he happened to be putting a trip together.

To give an example of what Don, boy population expert, often faces in this country, this trip quickly burgeoned from two persons

Looking for peace and tranquility in Tibet, I instead ran into Green Slime. Ganden monastery is in the background. We did not destroy it; the Chinese did.
[Carol Haslett photo]

to nine—but that was nothing. Once he organized a trip which, in three days of planning, mushroomed from two people to twenty-one.

Through Don, I was introduced to the Natahala Outdoor Center bunch which consisted of roughly half the tourist population of Kathmandu. Don called a meeting for the trip and we carefully hashed out logistics:

"OK! Who spelled porridge?"

"Why?"

"It's spelt, p-o-r-a-g-e."

"What's wrong with that?"

"It's p-o-r-i-d-g-e."

"No, there's two r's—"

"OK! That takes care of food. What about a first-aid kit?"

"I gotta prayer wheel."

"Hey, they sell some great codeine here at the Chemist's."

"What about rapids? How hard's this river we're running?"

"I don't know," Don said.

"What do you mean you don't know?"

"Well, how am I supposed to know the difficulty of the rapids when I don't know what river we're running?"

"Huh?"

"Listen: America's the land of opportunity; Nepal's the land of options. I haven't decided yet."

"Why do I even hang around with this crowd?" someone muttered.

"Because it's cheaper," someone else answered.

The lack of a river was really a moot point because I still lacked a boat. Fortunately, kayaks and paddles were[1] abundant in Kathmandu and easy to procure, thanks to the expeditions that had come to Nepal, scared the daylights out of themselves, and immediately abandoned their boats, kayaking, baths, and all water-oriented activities.

The first two boats I found were Holoforms. One had a seat but no footrests; the other had footrests but no seat. Both were missing their walls.

"Any wall?" I asked the Nepali whose lone purpose in life was to watch these two boats.

"Walls?"

"Made of ethafoam, like this," I said, pointing to the seat.

"You have right there."

"Yeah, on the seat. I'd like walls. They go here."

"We don't have."

"Know where I can get some?"

"America."

This mad-hatter style of conversation went on for ten minutes when suddenly the Nepali disappeared into a shed and returned, triumphantly, with a sheet of inch-thick ethafoam.

"Too thin," I said.

"You glue together."

"Where can I get glue?"

"America."

He returned to the shed, and I was hoping he would postpone his suicide, when suddenly he reemerged with the two missing walls.

"Maybe these will work," he said, his voice still filled with dejection.

Since necessity is the unwed mother of improvisation, I began to outfit myself. Learning the happy Asiatic disorder of proceedings,

_____

[1] 1986

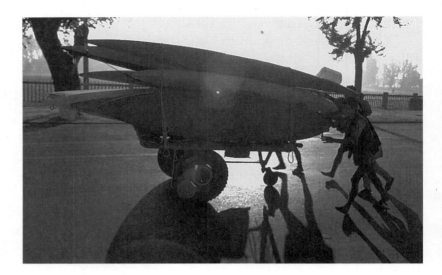

Out of our four months in Nepal, we spent three shuffling boats around Kathmandu.

I set out. For starters I immediately discovered that I could get by on just two words of Nepali: *kay garnee*, meaning, "Do you take Visa?"

Quickly, I became the envy of the group.

"Where did you get that wool sweater?" they asked.

"It's not a wool sweater, it's a pile jacket."

"And that rain coat?"

"You mean my paddle jacket? Do you need glasses?"

"And those tennis shoes?"

"Those happen to be my river boots. You really should have your eyes checked."

"How about that insulite pad?"

"That's my flotation."

"And those garbage sacks!"

"River bags."

"And they're filled with garbage. How about that!"

"That's my camping gear."

I was ready. All that I needed was a river.

At this point, I'd like to highlight the fact that, at the time, it was in vogue to be climbing the Himalayas without oxygen. So let me humbly assert that the various groups of people I ran rivers with over the ensuing months, *all did so without the aid of oxygen.* Some of us even tipped over. No, if climbers really want to make a big deal about something then they should go scale their mountains under the influence of nitrous oxide. (". . . suddenly Reinhold stopped giggling and, as he gasped, he pointed desperately at the valve on his nitrous oxide bottle. We began to snicker. 'Please, help me!' he managed to mutter as we began laughing ourselves (sic). Tears froze on my face. As he sank down in the snow where we abandoned him we broke into hysterics. It all seemed so funny at the time . . . .")

Meanwhile, through a complicated process involving a bottle of rum and the position of the moon and stars, Don chose the Seti, a river named after the legendary Abominable Riverman. This river starts by draining the flanks of some really high mountains that are perpetually hidden in the clouds. Everyone makes a really, really big deal out of the mountains, although they also make a big deal about the view-obstructing clouds. This is because they have spent hundreds of dollars getting to Nepal and jeopardized their jobs by taking time off to do so; they are not about to admit, after all the effort, that they didn't see diddly squat because of a weather eclipse. Anyway, hidden in the mountains, the Seti drops approximately six miles to the foot. In Pokhara, however, it flattens out enough for everyone to throw their garbage in it, then it goes underground. As you can see, it's a river that has something for everyone—so long as you like free-falling, garbage collecting, and spelunking. Yet from where it re-emerges—except for one purported tight spot—the river was supposed to behave itself.

Don rented us a minibus, and, as I quickly discovered, getting to or from most of Nepal's runs involves a mandatory pass through the disease-depot of Muggling. The road to it is as crooked as a roomful of insurance agents; however, it wouldn't be half as dangerous if the Nepalese would only put turn signals on their water buffaloes. As for Muggling itself: Stay awhile and you'll certainly leave with a fatal ailment. Only scatologists should venture out into its back lanes.

We arrived at our put-in late in the day and camped. The following morning, all the local villagers emptied out to watch us leave. They had good reason, too, for just downstream—out of sight from our camp—lived a steep, jagged rock drop. They were there in happy anticipation of witnessing a disaster. This, we figured, was the tight spot. If the villagers were disappointed that we walked this rapid, they were good sports and didn't show it, and instead helped us to portage the fully laden raft.

Beyond, the river widened. The water was warm, the day was pleasant, and I would even have dozed off if the occasional rock

being thrown hadn't aroused me. An even ruder awakening awaited downstream where the current suddenly heaved itself into a giant blossoming cushion right in front of me. A scout revealed the river sloughing off to the right into a pool, then taking a hard left shot down a bedrock alley. A human skull and bones littered our vantage point—a bad omen, I reckoned. Don however, took no notice. Although he had never been in the Peace Corps, he has that half-glass-full-of-water approach and immediately spotted the appropriate run. Not that I thought the glass was half-empty, I just thought it was half-full of giardia and plague and cholera and hoof-in-mouth and dyslexia and diptera and what-not.

I immediately spotted the walk.

Readers: "Don't you mean, diphtheria?"

"Yes, that, too."

We reasoned that this was probably the tight spot, and we relaxed. But several hundred unseen yards downstream, waiting, was an insidious hole, which our neophyte member, Robin, unwillingly dropped into.

Robin, a friend of Don's, had come to Nepal to learn to white-water kayak—an excellent place to learn because, if he failed, one more corpse in a tributary of the Ganges wasn't going to disturb anyone. Now Robin's modus operandi so far was, when tipping over, to bang on the bottom of his boat with his hands and someone would nose their boat up to him, allowing him to lever himself upright. In five miles of river, Robin not only had logged more upside-down yardage than most boaters accumulate in a lifetime but he'd also beaten out more drum solos than Gene Krupa. Since Robin had an incredible ability to hold his breath for long periods, we had not failed him. But now there was Robin in that hole—at least there was an occasional glimpse of Robin's *boat* in that hole. Robin banged not so patiently on his hull waiting for someone, *anyone*. His banging increased to war-beat tempo. But we all accidentally washed past him and even if it had been on purpose I couldn't have blamed us. Robin swam.

The following day, after passing through a steep, green-walled gorge, we came to Damauli. Originally we had planned to buy a few vegetables here to supplement our vast supplies. We were all extremely seasoned outdoor people. In fact, not only did we have infinite knowledge of planning, we also had with us two California rafters who knew everything there was to know in the universe.[2] In

◀ Don Weeden, dealing with the Seti, taking time off from his job—passing out condoms.

———

[2] Or at least had an opinion on it.

Kathmandu, using our wealth of wisdom, we had bought food that was to last *at least* six days: In those first two days we had demolished our supplies. Damauli saved us.

From Damauli down, the river divorced the road once more, the current issuing us through a pleasant valley—at least, pleasant for all except Robin. Robin was still absorbed in his self-inflicted accelerated learning pace. I'd already lost count of his tipovers. I'd seen more of Robin's hands banging on his hull than I'd seen of his face. Robin's hull had presented itself to the sky so often I got worried the UV might be damaging it. That evening around the fire there was a communal lament that we had not tied fish hooks to Robin's helmet; we could have been devouring fresh fish for dinner.

And it was at this camp where a specific trait developed that let our group know we were, without a doubt, in Nepal. Locally known as, *disaa logio*, the basic symptoms begin in the lower digestive tract, rendering a weak stool which is immediately accompanied by a strong squat. Nepal is not a place where one can live without quantities of medicine. Here, even the most holistic person quickly loses faith as they sprint behind the nearest bush. Fortunately, chemical warfare is cheap at local pharmacies—like the anti-giardia Tiniba, a toxin so lethal it kills small rodents within fifty feet of its user.

On the evening of the fifth day, we entered the Trisuli and floated to its sacred confluence with the Kali Gandaki. Here, a funeral was finishing; the corpse, wrapped in cloth, was laid in a shallow trench at the water's edge and boulders were mounded on top of it. These river-side funerals cleanse the deceased person's soul but I don't think they'll ever catch on in the States. I can just imagine the rangers on the Colorado: "OK everyone! We'd like you to pee in the water, pack all your garbage and fecal matter out and make sure you bury your dead below the high water mark with at least a hundred rocks on top of them."

Being polite, we had to wait for the funeral to end before Don could hire the hearse, a local truck, to take us back to Kathmandu.

Waiting for the next river trip to commence, I attempted to learn all I could about Nepal. For example, being thorough and unselective, I learned the King's name: His Majesty Maharajadhiraja Birendra Bir Bikram Shah Dev. He's not someone you want to get behind in line when he's signing ten-dollar traveler's checks. He stands at the wheel of the lone Hindu monarchy. (This is always followed by "on earth," leading me to believe it may not be the lone Hindu monarchy in the *universe*.) King M Bx3 S D pastes his mug on his country's money and, just to show how confident he is of his face, he keeps his own stash in a Swiss bank account. Rumors of corruption are only that and (as the maimed of Kathmandu will attest) so are the rumored bombs that occasionally go off, planted by those not in on the various skims. But hey, what the heck? The country's buses run. Some even leave on time and, occasionally, those that don't drive over a cliff actually arrive at their destinations.

There are more guidebooks written about the country than Bibles ever printed. Yet what is really needed is an epicure's directory to Kathmandu. There you can enjoy every ethnic kind of culinary poisoning. In fact the Guillain-Barré melted over sastrugi was the best I've ever had.

Readers: "OK, that's enough, get on with the rivers, would you!"

Which brings me to the Sun Kosi.

Whether it really is or not, the Sun Kosi seems to be a major Himalayan drainage. It draws from Tibet, takes a hard left in Nepal, and picks up all sorts of little Kosis on the way to the Terai.

This ten-day trip was run by the Natahala Outdoor Center, and officially guided by Arlene Burns and Kiwi Dave Allardice—along with a plethora of unofficial guides. The guide-to-client ratio on this trip was roughly forty to one. Carol and I were allowed to tag along by the good graces of N.O.C. and its clients.

We put in near Lamusangu, upstream of Dolalghat. Here, the rapids were not big, but within a day the river began showing muscle. At our first camp a man approached us with a swollen arm so infected his fingers looked like teats on a cow udder. One of the clients dug out some penicillin and Arlene, in broken Nepali, explained the pill-swallowing schedule. Afterwards, I'm sure the patient went home and, following Arlene's pantomime, touched all the pills to his arm and circled one fist around the other, to mock the earth's rotation. Then, in one fell swoop, he probably popped all forty pills.

The following day we passed through some hearty water which brought us to the junction of the Rosi Kosi. It was not a name to ignore. Since it was another sacred confluence it was marked by a grave, which was discovered by one of the unofficial guides who, while resting in an eddy, looked up and found himself stared back at by a decomposing face. No matter. Despite not eating for the remainder of the trip and attending therapy for the rest of his life, there was to soon be compensation for the death.

Close by was a temple dedicated to a *lingam*, a phallic-shaped rock worshiped by those praying for pregnancy. Judging by the pile of marigolds offered to this stone, a local population boom—without the Pope's help—was imminent. It's a pity high school kids in the U.S. aren't warned to avoid contact with such lewd rocks. ("I told you, Susan, I don't want you dating Jimmy. He's got a big lingam in the trunk of his car.") I wanted to stay longer but a local woman began eyeing my kayak with a specific twinkle in her eye.

In time we came to Meatgrinder. Viewed from above, it was an ominous horizon line. Viewed from below it felt like a bottle of Rolaids. The fresh creation of this rapid, like many of the Sun Kosi's other drops, can be attributed directly to excessive lingam adulation. In other words, without the people overwhelming and collapsing the ecosystem, the river wouldn't be half as fun. If you wish to see the Himalayas in their current state, you had better do so quickly. They are washing away. Nepal's new location will soon be out in the Bay of Bengal.

Besides Meatgrinder, the only other immediate danger threatening the group was Dave, who nearly killed the entire party by feeding Vegemite to several locals one day at lunch. Dave, for reasons that are not scientifically explainable, decided to conduct a taste test and feed various luncheon foods to unsuspecting and innocent Nepali subjects. All proceeded well as they merrily gobbled down our cheeses and bread and nuts and chocolate and biscuits. Then it happened. From his private stash, he began slipping them crackers desecrated with Vegemite. Immediately, there were three Nepalese grasping their throats and writhing on the ground.

Although Dave wouldn't admit he had done it, we discovered the open jar of Vegemite and quickly raised the alarm. "Dave's poisoned the natives! Pack your boats!"

"Run for it!" someone yelled.

"If the village finds out we've all had it!" someone else hollered.

What ensued was a scene like the British leaving Dunkirk. We covered roughly ninety miles that afternoon and camped on the opposite side of the river, silent and well-hidden.

Later, under blackout conditions, Dave muttered "How could they not like Vegemite? I just don't understand. That's the only thing my parents ever fed me when I was growing up."

"Then that explains the damage to your judgment," returned a voice from the dark.

Farther down we came to the Harkapurs: One, Two, and Three. Three, once considered the hardest on the river, was a needle route between an osterizing hole and a wall that the current railroaded into—a place where people saw God, broke their ankles, or did both. But the monsoons had temporarily remodeled it into a straight, unobstructed float.

Eventually, time and rapids smeared across one large pallet of events. But the Jungle Corridor, a series of back-to-back drops, stood out more than any other event on the trip. It was the most consistent and fun (and, thanks to global warming, *warm*) big water I've ever paddled. But, like the trip, it was over all too soon. The trip itself took ten days and ended abruptly when the river

With the current rate of Nepal's erosion, there is little need to climb the Himalayas. Here we are camped on what was most likely, two thousand years before, the top of Mount Everest.

veered towards India, issuing out onto the Terai. The hills that had bullied it suddenly stopped, and the change from three-dimensional land to two-, was like coming out of a movie theater into blinding daylight.

Three days later we were headed for the Marsyandi river, where Don was joining us once more. For this trip, we rented two Land Rovers and, once more, followed the dreaded road to the Seti. But at Dumre we turned onto a goat path that the locals insisted was a road. Our drivers pretended it wasn't, insisting on more money and threatened to turn back. Don placated them until we reached Bhote Odar. He had run the upper Marsyandi many years before. He remembered that it was a great run but the rest of his memories were scattered. He proposed a two-hour hike to a town named something like Phillet-Mignon.

About two-thousand feet above sea level, Phillet-Mignon was perched on two cliffs that nearly touched above the river. The surrounding valley was lush and open (a travel book euphemism for

Greystoke providing ferry service on the Sun Kosi. Few bridges span the 170 miles of river, resulting in numerous dumb hit songs to be written about tragic, cross-river love affairs.

mosquito overcrowding). A flat and milky blue water awaited us below the village. Where the cliffs fell back, the river quickened; the tongues were brisk, the gradient was snappy, the holes were plentiful, and the eddy lines were sharp. Our group was cocky. All was well with the world until a long drop, beginning with a chipper class 3, which steepened into a die-hard 4. There were three people in front of me, but as the rapid hardened they sort of disappeared. Then, from the corner of my eye, I saw Don harbored snugly in an eddy by the bank. He was waving his paddle at me—a mere courtesy at this point; he'd been trying to warn me that my course was not healthy, which I soon saw, too, but I was not going to be given a vote in changing. The river narrowed, delivering me into a deep, thundering, river-wide hole. The last thing I saw was a magnificent upside-down view of the Himalayas: the clouds, for a moment, had come off of them. But by the time the river had performed a Heimlich maneuver on me and spit me out, the clouds were hiding the mountains once more. Later, Don sidled up to me and said, "Oh yes, *now* I remember where that rapid was."

From Bhote Odar down *was* some of the best paddling in the world (something I can claim because the river is now dammed). Later, after the run but before the dam, I talked to the project engineer who explained the dam's logistics. He made this easier by clarifying the logistics of another dam, one proposed for the Karnali in West Nepal. His government, he explained, wanted to build a dam where the river issues into the Terai. A Japanese firm was trying to secure the contract to build a two-hundred-meter concrete dam. But a conglomerate Norwegian and Australian firm maintained that a lower earth-filled dam would be better suited to the earthquake-prone region. The choice is not made by the Nepalese but by the World Bank (with major funding from Saudi Arabia and Kuwait) which finances the loans—but only after a Canadian firm runs a study to determine the better of the two projects. Still, the dam can't be built until India agrees to buy a portion of the power. And all this must be coordinated from a country whose phones don't work. Until then I'd thought nothing in the world was more complicated than the rules to cricket.

December came and Carol and I stepped over the border into Darjeeling[3] to clear our passports. We returned to Nepal for one last river, the Kali Gandaki, Nepal's little Ganges. If you are dead, people will carry you for miles just to burn or bury you next to it.

---

[3] Or, if you're dyslexic, Geedarling.

The two-day trek to the Kali. Actually it could have taken one but our enterprising porters soaked us for all we were worth.

---

[4] We hired them just for the gag.

Or, for a discount funeral, they will give you a simple heave-ho into this fastlane to deliverance.

From Pokhara, Dave Allardice, Carol, and myself caught a bus to Nandanda, from which it was a one-day-spread-over-two-day hike to Kusma and the river. Dave's Nepali had supposedly improved since the Sun Kosi, so we let him hire our porters, Poosh and Shiv. At first they wanted to negotiate separately but after three hours of bargaining Poosh came to Shiv[4] and we had to give in and accept their price, one reserved "especially for us."

Just before Kusma we crossed the Modi Khola, a small technical stream, and since there was a checkpost at Kusma and we had no trekking permits, we put in here to save some baksheesh. A rocky, technical mile delivered us to the Kali, which met us with a robust flow—but it wasn't half as robust as the stench. At the confluence were sixteen rotting bodies each lying under its own mound of boulders, each one with its own set of vultures sitting patiently on top, all evilly hunched over with their grease-trap necks. As I put the borrowed boat down and sat on it, the boat's wall slipped and it caved-in like a cheap suitcase. The vultures suddenly regarded me with renewed interest, certain I was next, certain that I would be pinned in my kayak.

Besides the Kali's holiness, the river used to be a main salt route from Tibet to India.[5] It drains from the Mustang region and is a foremost pass through the Himalayas. Traders have followed it for so long that their footsteps, not the river, have carved the pass through the mountains. (Where the traders got their pepper is unknown.)

The river began with pools and drops. The drops proved straightforward, but the route-finding was hard until we were in them. Dave didn't hesitate at anything dubious; meet Dave and you meet a Kiwi. Equipment and skill eternally live in the shadow of blind faith. He only scouted as a humorous hindsight to see where he should have gone.[6]

The sun was somewhere overhead, but it played hide and seek behind the hills leaving us in shadows, and with the shadows came chilling whiffs of breeze. We set up camp—a matter of laying our sleeping bags on the sand. By the time we had built a fire, dusk had closed in; by the time we had finished cooking, it was totally dark. Lying on our beach we watched the odd twinkling of lamps on the layered hillsides and followed them up until they melted into a twinkling of stars. Carol said, "It sure is black." I fell asleep, and the next thing I knew the sky was on fire and people were yelling. A hut directly across from us was busily burning down. We watched silhouetted figures dashing around and throwing green banana leaves on adjacent huts trying to keep the sparks at bay. The hut collapsed in an explosion of sparks, followed by dying flames and outlines of the dispossessed, then quiet and darkness.

The next day we entered a river-smoothed, marbled gorge where no sunlight had ever penetrated. Along the walls were small grottos of fern. Pigeons in dire need of a statue circled overhead,

[5] The literal translation of this pass is "Pass the salt."

[6] *White Water Nepal*, by Peter Knowles and Dave Allardice. 1992 Rivers Publishing U.K. and Menasha Ridge Press, U.S.A.

but even they were in shadow. A cold eeriness permeated the scene. J.R.R. Tolkien, who once lived up the Modi Kola, must have seen this gorge and been inspired to write: " . . . And the little twerp Hobbit asked the three bears, 'OK! Which one of you spelled porridge?'"

Eventually, we approached a rapid where a body was being burned. The route seemed obvious but I hesitated and Dave, seeing that I was going to look, also waited. A good thing, too, although I don't think the Nepalis would have minded Carol and me chucking a freshly dead Dave into their funeral pyre—that is, if the river-centered hole he would have dropped into had ever released him from eternal circulation. A simple cut right solved the route. As we ran, the small crowd of mourners that were gathered around the body abandoned it and rushed to the bank to watch us. If this wasn't a cultural intrusion, I didn't know what was. A chilling breeze blew up the valley, the fire was at its height, and amidst the flames lay the charred body, on its back with its knees up and its arms folded over its chest. All I could think of was Sam McGee,

The only known picture of Dave Allardice scouting a drop.

A Badi Gad woman taking wild liberties with me as she fingerpaints my forehead with a teka. [Carol Haslett photo]

and as we floated quietly past we all lamented that we could not warm up around the fire.

In time we reached the confluence of the Badi Gad. A small village and a temple garnished the rock above these two rivers. A Bubba heartily welcomed us, showed us his temple, blessed us with tekas,[7] and proceeded to feed us some mushy gray matter. None of us could guess its original identity. Dave offered a consoling thought that whatever the lethal effect might be, at least we were now blessed.

Downstream came a long, washed-out paddle—exactly what we expected for the remainder of the trip. But the village of Rani Ghat changed the agenda. Here in the midst of nowhere sat an abandoned mansion, its architecture a blend of Roman, Colonial, and Nepalese styles. Several temples decorated the garden. Broad, low-step stairs flanked by brick led to a grand porch supported by two-story cement columns. The mansion's gutted spaciousness screamed royalty. Out back were a kitchen and maid's quarters. The only inhabitants I found were weeds growing from the cracks in the cement and plaster.

A wash separated this villa from a village where, by contrast, all the buildings were made of mud, sticks, and rock. One of the locals spoke as much English as Dave did Nepali and, after an exchange in broken hunks, our inquiries about the mansion were

---

[7] Red paint smeared between the eyes. I can't help but think of them as targets for riot police.

The mansion in the middle of nowhere.

met with amazing information. The place, which had been lived in only three days ago had housed several thousand people. This, however, undercut the next statistic; assuming the several thousand had helped build it, the task had taken a mere seven hours.

Dave inquired about buying eggs.

"Have dock's eggs," the person answered.

"Dogs' eggs?" exclaimed Dave, pointing to a sleeping dog.

"Docks. Docks!" said the Nepali, starting to laugh uncontrollably.

"Dogs?"

"Docks!"

"Ducks!"

The joke carried quickly and runners were immediately dispatched to neighboring villages to spread it. People began streaming in from the hills to hear it. Carol, Dave, and I quickly left, but already the joke had traveled downstream.

It preceded us back to Kathmandu, where a national holiday

was called in its honor. Carol, Dave, and I were offered Nepali citizenship. Carol and I graciously declined, but occasionally I hear that Dave is still considering the offer. I think that first he had better swear off Vegemite.

Dave Allardice. Although it looks like he might be swearing off Vegemite, he is not. He is about to slap a mosquito on one of our porters.

BRITAIN

Ruling What Waves?

Here various thoughts blended and tumbled about in the mind most disorderly. To leave this quiet bank and willingly rush out, in cold blood, into a field of white breakers; to tarnish the fair journey with a foolhardy prank; to risk the Rob Roy where the touch of one rock was utter destruction. Will it be pleasant? Can it be wise?
Is it right?

—John MacGregor, *A Thousand Miles in the Rob Roy Canoe*, 1881

❖   ❖   ❖

When I left Seattle it was raining. When I arrived in London it was still raining. Small world.

Bravely, I'd flown to London. I emphasize bravely, because even Sylvester ("Steroid Breath") Stallone had called a major press conference to cancel his London trip, due to threatened terrorism. Distressed that I wouldn't get to see him, I nevertheless outlined two movie scenarios for him. Because of logistical problems, however, he will only be able to complete one.

SCENARIO #1: *Rambo V: Rambo Rains over London*

For two hours straight, with no plot in sight, Rambo relentlessly battles, maims, shoots, and splatters an evil consortium of fanatical Iranians; pro-Qadhafi, pro-football players; KGB, PKK, PVC, IRA, IRS and NOW agents—right up to the final scene where he narrowly escapes them all by diving out of a helicopter over London, only to discover his parachute is really a bmob packed by a dyslexic terrorist, and, much to the relief of movie goers world-wide, Rambo permanently joins the ionosphere. Of course, the alternative is:

SCENARIO #2: *Rocky MXII: The Final Blow*

In this, Good Ol' Rocky raises his dukes against the forces of villainy only to find out in the thirty-fourth round he is faced off against one of his (thinly disguised) ex-girlfriends, a suicide bomber, who not only packs a roll of nickels in her left but twenty-two pounds of contact explosives in what proves to be a dynamite right . . . .

In time, Dave Manby fetched me safely from the airport—and no doubt an impending bomb attack. Thankful to be alive, we quickly descended upon the nearest pub, "Ye Olde Manure and Shovel," to celebrate.

Dave said, "I'll bet you're hungry," and ordered something that came in glasses and looked like sci-fi sludge from a septic tank. Of course, not wanting to make fun of any strange "fur'in" customs, I said nothing and ate up.

Lunch gone, Dave said, "I'll bet you're thirsty now," and he ordered us something to wash it down which I swear looked exactly like what we just ate.

"Bet you're hungry again, aren't you?" he asked when I was through washing down lunch—and, well, when we at last saw daylight once more, I wasn't hungry or thirsty and London had this *fuzzy* look to it. Maybe it was the sentiment I felt for the place, or maybe it was just the sediment.

After driving in circles we arrived in Whitechapel, one of London's high-rent districts. I'm glad, because I would have hated to see the poor neighborhood. Supposedly, Jack the Ripper used to range in the district, however, this was hard to swallow since there was no fog. The anarchists used to try and unite in these parts, too, but it didn't work. Dave said there wasn't any more anarchy but this was an outright lie because when we entered his flat, anarchy was doing just fine. Dave merrily informed me that for four quid a week, split with his flatmates,[1] you couldn't expect much; however, by the looks of things, I thought four quid was excessive and I told him so.

---

[1] Bubble and Squeak.

But he shrugged and said, "You're ignoring the advantages—like the electric bill. There isn't one." And I could see immediately why there wasn't: A double-ought wire was bypassing the meter, which explained the five electric heaters glowing nonstop. What the other advantages to the place were, Dave never got around to telling me, and I never did get around to figuring out.

In the kitchen, domestic and benign Petri dish cultures had escaped and, finding lush natural habitat, had gone wild across the counter[2] and into the sink and up the mountain of dishes. The kitchen was not a place you wanted to wander into at night without strong light and a large stick. The mountain of dishes could actually grow taller, and occasionally did, only to be leveled off by kayaks being passed through the shattered (no one had bothered to

_____
[2] Yet another Whitechapel counter-culture.

111

open it) kitchen window to and from the back yard. Needless to say, that the state of the kitchen was typical of the flat.

The next day, thinking about all the things England has given the world—Beatle haircuts, spinning cue balls, football riots, the latest developments in dysfunctional royalty, and—as I stepped off the curb and nearly got run over, the right-hand drive—I set off to see London. However, I immediately discovered that the city was built from the blueprint of a maze and I got hopelessly lost. There were your usual pigeons interacting with the local statues (Hardy, I doubt, would have kissed Nelson) and soot-covered antiquities being stared at by herds of milling and rather confused-looking tourists. Yet, what caught my eye were the billboards. They were advertising condoms so big they would fit the London Underground.

That night I gave a slide show to the River Rats, a group dedicated to international kayaking. Dave, had foolishly asked me if I needed any props, and I had foolishly answered that a couple of pigs would do nicely. Finding several for hire, he had spent the day filling out stacks of papers so he could transport them across London, and a special form so he could cross Tower Bridge. In the end, however, the R.S.P.C.A., naturally concerned for the welfare of pigs in such suspicious company, called up the unsuspecting pub and asked if this was the place where the pigs were being delivered. To which they replied: "You can tell that bunch that if any pigs show up here tonight they'll never use this pub again for their shows."

The next day I caught a train to Scotland to give another show and to find out more pertinent facts about the country—like how come no one riots at cricket matches?[3] First, it was imperative that I learn the language. Contrary to popular belief, English is not spoken in Britain. I mean, when a tire loses its air, we don't say, "Damn it! I've got another apartment!" Opportunity for misunderstanding is fertile soil. Take for example this misinterpreted situation:

Open-minded American: "Waiter, I'd like to try something positively British. What do you recommend?"

Waiter: "Why don't you try our spotted dick." [4]

Open-minded and now also standing up beet-red American with fists clenched: "WHAT DID YOU SAY! APOLOGIZE TO MY WIFE!"

It is easy to see how *Alice's Adventures in Wonderland* came to be written here. Just take these examples in whitewater: Fiberglass is "glassfibre." A paddle jacket is an "anorak." An endo is a "loop."

---

3 Because they are all asleep.

4 It nests in old-growth restaurants.

Shuttles are "ferries." Holes are "stoppers." An eddy turn is a "break out." A kayak is a "canoe," a canoe is a "canadian," and what they call Canadians I never found out—but I'm sure a Canadian wouldn't like it. And in British tradition, the sport has been dissected and categorized right down to the rip cord on a spraydeck—"a becket." (Fatality report: "The victim obviously drowned because of his failure to correctly identify his becket.")

We were speeding north out of Aberdeen in a Mini, and a boater by the name of Jim was driving. He had a last name but he was driving too fast for me to catch it. Some of the scenery was to be expected, such as hills covered with gorse and broom; other scenery was not like where the gloaming had all been plowed under for row after regimented row of tax-write-off larch and pine. After racing a lorry (translation: slow truck) and beating it to a one-lane bridge which it sideswiped, we crossed the river Spey. Why anyone would name a river after an operation to remove ovaries was beyond me. Not only does it demonstrate what sort of tastes these locals possess, but it also shows their lax disregard for proper spelling.

Jim said, "You should paddle the Spey."

"Good water?"

"No, but at the take-out there's a distillery and they give you free drink."

But crossing the Spey brought up a subject far more confusing than scores of cricket matches: trespass laws. The Spey had been a watershed (no pun intended) trespass case brought forth by boater Clive Freshwater (also no pun intended) whose presence the river owners protested. The legal battle ascended to the House of Lords; which is just like the U.S. Supreme Court, where the members take turns napping, except in Britain they wear funny wigs while doing so. To keep the members awake, Clive argued that Spey navigation rights had been established by the timber rafts that were floated down it decades ago; most of the wood going for various British war efforts. Crucial testimony came from an old woman who remembered seeing these rafts. Clive won, which just goes to show that even if the British didn't do all that well in their wars, the populace—in the end—did win access to some of their own rivers.

In Scotland, there is no trespass law, but an owner has the right to ask you to leave, which means you can trespass as long as you don't get *caught* trespassing. In any case, no one has yet broken the news to the Scots, whose policy has always been to roam the land at will, whether some snot-nosed prince tells them to leave or not.

At last we arrived at our river, the Findhorn. We put in at Randolph's Leap, a narrow slot where the English had chased yet another free-roaming Scot, supposedly one Randolph. Although the English might have been good runners, they lacked jumping skills, and here Randolph had parted company with them. Whether Randolph was a good jumper isn't mentioned, for if he wasn't he at least had to have been a good swimmer. Whether Randolph's name was Randolph is doubtful, too, since the English never caught him to find out. (Besides, he was probably carrying phony ID.) In any case, it was not a drop our group wanted to swim through, so we put in below it.

The Findhorn was, and I imagine still is, a small river cutting through a black rock gorge. The water was peat brown, almost as dark as the rock that taunts it. Upstream, the river oozes from a waterlogged bog; that makes the river's level hard to predict since the bog, acting as a sponge, releases water when it damn well feels like it. At first I thought the water tasted of unborn whisky but as we descended, those who tipped over started doing so with alarming frequency, and I began to doubt the water's innocence.

It hadn't rained for several days but the level was up to a medium flow. For the 57th parallel and the end of November, the temperature was unseasonably warm. Overhead, a business-like wind sped across the gorge but only little puffs of it spiraled down on us.

The first and biggest consequential rapid was Chicane, a steep drop, perhaps a total of ten feet. A major hole that could be skirted right or left commanded the width of the river. Right spit you into a vigorous eddy directly above another hole with a tough ferry to avoid it. Left hurried you into a boulder offering only a small cushion to bounce off, stopping all much-needed momentum down the next piece of vertical that carried through some unstable slaps but happily by-passed the second hole.

Next came several stair-stepping but straight rapids, then the last major drop, a *wee* slot—a good place for Randolph—where almost the entire river funneled down a five-foot-wide tongue. Attacked wrong, the drop's plunge liked to bury back decks popping half the participants for a highland fling.

At the take-out, the black walls suddenly gave way to outcrops of red sandstone. Until I ran the Findhorn I was under the impression that every inch of river had been explored in Britain, but in Scotland, this was not the case. With the onslaught of plastic boats there were still a few steep rocky creeks waiting to be descended. Since they issue from the erratic, water-releasing bogs, the timing to run them is difficult to predict.

From Aberdeen I traveled to Cardiff ("Hey waiter! There's a hare in my welsh rabbit!") then back to London, where Dave said, "I'll bet you're hungry." Over the ensuing glasses of lunch, I mentioned trespass law, only to discover that if I thought I had all that sorted out, I was severely mistaken. Scottish law does not apply to Wales and England, and, basically, boaters in these latter two divisions are lower than—and have the same rights as—toe jam. The plot thickens.

So just pretend I never went to Scotland and let me start again. (Complaints of any factual discrepancy in the following material should be addressed to the Guinness company.)

Britain: Ruling What Waves?

Kayaking may not have a history in America but it has one in Great Britain. His name is John MacGregor. MacGregor, who lived in the mid-1800s, dubbed his kayaks "Rob Roys." They were of featherlight oak construction—a mere ninety pounds—and with them he toured Europe, the Baltic, and the Middle East. Making his observations through blue spectacles, he boated in plus fours, a frock coat with six pockets, and a straw hat; he carried a Bible, flew a Union Jack on his deck, and liked to stand in his boat while singing *Rule Britannia*. This Great White knucklehead referred to his boat and himself as "we," to his boat as "she," then proceeded to sleep with it. So what does this have to do with river rights in England and Wales? Absolutely nothing.

Today, there are an estimated 100,000 paddlers in Britain—more than one paddler per square mile of country. There are more than five hundred clubs (but probably very few members are current on their dues so a lot of good that statistic is). Yet, surprisingly, few good whitewater rivers are available to the masses. Due to lack of river access, most of the good rivers can't be run. Not only does the riparian owner own the adjoining river bank (and probably the nearest financial bank as well), but they also own the bed of the river and the water passing over it. Unless there's a public right of navigation, they own that too, along with the right to take fish, and most likely the air above the river, along with any satellites, planets, and galaxies passing over.

It is a class problem ingrained in English tradition, going back to little Willy Shakespeare poaching some nobleman's deer. Imagine some tweed-coated, aristocratic fisherman contentedly casting his fly into a pastoral river. It is his God-given right to play with his fly in such a manner, and he can do what he likes with it. But if he is so foolish to let a maid get caught playing with *his* fly and the tabloids get a hold of it (the scandal, not his fly), then the GNP of Britain doubles overnight. Back to our pastoral river, though. Introduce a group of non-paying, uninvited, unwashed, prank-playing, fun-loving, brightly colored but non color-coordinated boisterous kayakers floating into this picture and there goes the country swirling down the tube.

The British Canoe Union *Canoeing Handbook* states:

> "'Disturbance to fishing' can be a cause for legal proceedings in the civil courts and a case on the river Wharfe, which went to appeal, has set an unfortunate precedent in accepting that the passage of a canoe does disturb the right to fish even when no one is actually fishing."

Zealous fishermen also maintain that kayaks disturb the fish. But other than dynamite, I personally can't think of anything that disturbs a fish more than yanking it from the water by a hook through its face.

Gaining permanent access to Welsh and English rivers is a long, tedious process, much of it bogged down in the British tradition of councils, committees, and associations. And so enter CRACK. This is not your normal crack that sixth graders shoot each other over in the U.S., or even plumbers' crack, but CRACK, the Campaign for River Access for Canoes and Kayaks, a group that views the process of councils, committees, and associations like waiting for tortoises to mate. CRACK pledges[5] "more militant forms of action" to gain public access to Britain's rivers. After making fun of Sylvester Stallone, I apologize, face flushed with embarrassment, realizing it was most likely one of CRACK's pamphlets he got hold of, causing him to cancel his trip. CRACK

---

[5] Pledged. The outfit is now defunct.

promises: "A mass rally of canoeists will take place, possibly followed by a spontaneous act of defiance on a northern river where Canoeists are not welcome."

Such rallies are not new in Britain. In the 30s, the Ramblers, a hiking club, successfully carried out a similar mass trespass culminating in the "Access to the Countryside Act" that established a network of footpaths throughout Britain, and permitted the lower classes to use sidewalks.

If it can be proved that a river was once used for navigation, the rights to drift it can be established. Some claim that the access to rivers is guaranteed in the Magna Carta. CRACK claims rights on the Rivers Tee, Ribble, and Aire because the Romans navigated them, and the River Rye where barges were used to transport rock and logs for the Rievaulx Abbey (built in 1183). Unfortunately, the Romans were severely deficient in whitewater skills, which not only led to the fall of their empire but also means they set no precedent of running barge-loads of rock down good upper-grade waters in Britain.

A "spontaneous act of defiance" on the Seiont. Here, anti-trespass-law paddlers—after abseiling onto the river to gain access to it—challenge an "anti-poaching" barrier spontaneously erected the night before by anti-river-running fishermen. [Stuart Fisher photo]

In England and Wales, one does not merely wake up in the morning, observe a nice day and impulsively decide to go boating; that is, unless one wants to be chased by irate property holders. The system, however, can't be totally condemned; for insistent, pursuing landowners can be thanked personally for the informal yet extremely effective training of—so far—three British world slalom champions.

The *Canoeing Handbook* advises:

"Current practice on private waters is to seek the permission of known objectors. When planning a river trip, members should contact the relevant BCU advisor well in advance . . . . The river advisor will recommend if the trip should go ahead or not, and members must abide by what he or she says. An alternative time may be suggested, according to fishing season, or the fact that angling is better early and late in the day, by the frequency of other canoeing parties on the river, or by water levels. Advisors will give details of any agreements in force, and of persons to contact when prior application must be made for permissions. Advice may be given on access and egress points, and on the size and conduct of the party."

In short, the best time to paddle is never.

Just because paddlers are rarely allowed on hard rivers doesn't mean the sloughs and slow-and-stagnant back waters they are consigned to are not dangerous. Paddlers can be exposed to the obscure but serious Weil's disease, a bacterial infection carried in rat urine. The bacteria can be absorbed through the skin but more readily enters through a cut, and eventually it leads to kidney and liver failure. In one year there were sixty-one cases; most were sewer workers, but seven were boaters. I draw no connection between the two activities.

Another study concluded that by the time the Thames reaches London, its waters have passed through at least seven sets of kidneys—which is really a phenomenon, since the study reveals absolutely nothing about the water going through any other part of the digestive tract. As I was to learn, boaters don't approach each other in Britain and discuss water levels or even weather. Instead they say, "How many kidneys do you think the Thames goes through?" It was a hot discussion and once, as I listened to the dispute in which the number being argued bounced between thirteen and four, a person came up to me and, somewhat embarrassed, asked, "Does this sort of thing go on in the United States?"

"No," I answered. "The Thames doesn't flow through the United States."

Having gained a thorough grasp of British boating, along with a bad hangover, Dave and I headed for Llangollen (pronounced with a tubercular cough), the Dee river, and the annual Mike Jones Rally. Dave, extremely hard up for a speaker that year, had arranged for me to speak. The rally was Dave's brainchild, and its purpose was threefold: to honor the memory of Dave's friend who drowned on the Braldu, to gain access for all boaters, and to have a good laugh. Instead of washing his mountain of dishes Dave had, for ten years, annually waded through correspondence and made arrangements for river access, a lecture hall, shuttle service, fire-works, and camping; he had even harnessed divers (well, Dave didn't actually *harness* them, he just arranged for them) to rescue those swimming in the Town Falls rapid. The first year a hundred and fifty people attended, then three hundred the second year, seven hundred and fifty the third, and a thousand to fifteen hun-dred ever since. The organizing was finally passed on to a committee whose members acquired exclusive privileges, such as a legitimate reason not to wash their dishes.

The weekend event opened up sixteen miles of the Dee, including the most popular section, Horseshoe Falls to Llangollen. The 1961 *BCU Guide to the Waterways of the British Isles* warns:

> "From Horseshoe Falls [a weir] to Llangollen is generally regarded as too difficult . . . . From here it is best to transfer to the feeder canal . . . as the next two miles of river are extremely difficult—the fall is about 30 feet per mile . . . . If the river is attempted, over three hours should be allowed for the 2 miles as several sections require inspection. Difficulty IV . . . The Serpent's Tail. River narrows to about 5 feet and falls through a twisting chasm. Portage over rocks on left. Do not attempt to shoot unless you are sure of your technique."

Friday afternoon we spent putting up signs: Camping; No park-ing; No access. We even posted signs on the river bank above each rapid advising the boaters how they should run them. On Friday

Llangollen and the Jones Weekend by day; by night it felt more like Jonestown.

evening Dave made the rounds to landowners, a balancing act of diplomacy.

The next day, for all of Dave's organization, what ensued was good old-fashioned Whitechapel anarchy. At 8:00 I put on the river with a small group. Other groups were already ahead of us. Frost was still on the ground and the sweet smell of coal smoke permeated the air. I was hardly anxious to tip over as some were doing.

The river was hemmed in between a canal on one side (a

twenty-minute paddle back upstream if you didn't want to take the shuttle bus) and a resurrected steam railroad on the other. (Dave once tried to obtain this as a shuttle, but was defeated by regulations.) Since the trees had lost their leaves, there was an ample view of the hills: brown with bracken, checker-boarded with hedges, and dotted with sheep. One hill sheered into limestone cliffs; on another hill sat the ruins of some ancient castle. And as I gazed over the Welsh countryside, with the Dee flowing through it, I wondered: "Just how many kidneys has this river passed through so far?"

Our group took its time, other groups passed us, and soon there wasn't a vacant eddy. We reached Llangollen in an hour, the town abruptly walling in the river. A small but growing crowd gathered on the bridge—vultures watching tipovers. Already the harnessed divers were at work. Without them, swimmers would wash into the recycling weir immediately downstream.

By noon the invasion of the town was in full force. Cars with kayaks or racks on top of them had brought local traffic to a crawl; boats by the dozen lay scattered about the sidewalks, their dripping owners inside the pubs and cafes were busy water-staining the furniture. Drysuits, I'm sure, were not developed by boaters, but rather

Mike Jones Rally reenactment of the Titanic sinking.

by the establishment owners of Llangollen in a vain attempt to protect their property.

Returning upstream, we found that access onto the river was bottlenecked. People were climbing into boats as fast as they could. I think the idea was to get as many as possible on the river at one time to bring the water level up. Eddies were packed to capacity. The current turned into a never-ending unofficial parade of boats, most with someone in them. The Serpent's Tail was doing its best, however, to make boats and boaters part company. I wondered how many of those who swam ever saw their equipment again. The flotsam looked like a major maritime disaster in progress. Occasionally, a foolish, experienced boater ventured his nose into the Tail but inevitably failed to exit before someone landed in his lap.

This mayhem through the Serpent's Tail was further maximized by the chariot race (which had rules such as: "All competitors must abide by the Tacitus rules with the exception of rules MXVII, CMLXI, LXVIII, and MCMDIX which will apply if rule XVIII is accidentally broken." And entry form questions like: "What

Cardboard race from a past Mike Jones Ralley. (Jill Hodgshon & Pete Montgomery photo)

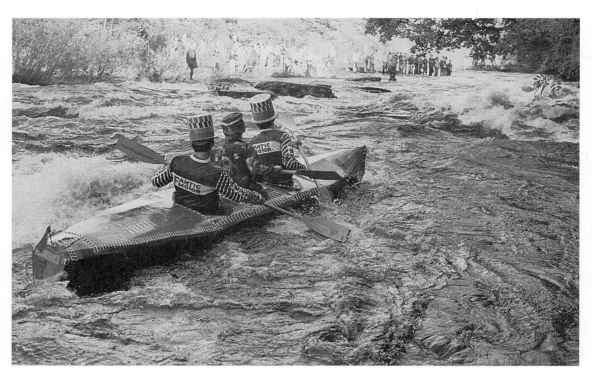

notable achievements have you been involved with prior to today's event?") This event had been tame compared to others in previous years which had seen an inflatable race (all competitors must interfere with other competitors) and a cardboard race, in which the boats could be of any design just so long as they were built solely from duct tape and cardboard.

With dusk came fervent pub activity, followed by a vague and puzzling slide show which caused a mass rush back to the pubs. I partook in this run on alcohol, and the effects of what I drank made me feel as if I were not participating in the Jones Weekend but rather in Jonestown itself. By midnight, drink had turned many of the alcohol enthusiasts into quadrupeds. The rally reached its unofficial finale at 2:00 a.m. when two well-oiled boaters in distress staggered into the police station and the following conversation ensued:

Boaters (desperately fighting gravity): "We need your help."

Constable (eyeing them suspiciously and answering tentatively): "Yes?"

Boaters: "We're booked into a bed and breakfast—"

Constable: "And wouldn't it be a good idea if you went there now?"

Boaters: "That's why we need your help. We can't find it."

Judging by the night's feverish activity—and the various puddles of what couldn't be consumed filling the gutters—I guessed that few people would be out early, especially since a cold, drizzly, Welsh rain had set in. But for many, it was their hungover mind over the irresistible matter of a river that might not be available until the next Jones Rally. At first light, the river began filling with boats. The colder the day grew, the more urgent the boating became. In the afternoon, trying to give statistical dimension to the mayhem, I visited the divers. They were jubilant because they had set a new record: They had just pulled out their two-hundredth victim. But at the First Aid shack, life had not been as exciting as expected. The only incidents worth mentioning were several head cuts, one requiring fourteen stitches, and three dislocated shoulders.

When the day was over I met Dave on the street. He said, "I'll bet you're hungry."

As we sipped dinner, all seemed right with the world. The festivities were subsiding, and a little Welsh village was returning to its peaceful, bucolic state. It was so quiet only the subtle ticking of a hidden bomb could be heard.

TURKEY

The Incomplete Thoughts of Whit Deschner

Never tell the truth unless one foot is in the stirrup.

—Turkish proverb

✦ ✦ ✦

At the end of the eighties, Turkey was liberally basting itself trying to attract the Common Market's attention—and Europe magnanimously ignored it. Yet, Turkey duly celebrated every little notch toward its goal as a major victory. When I arrived (as if that had everything to do with it) Lloyd's had just raised the insurance ranking of the national airline, thus decreasing the rates—a major deciding criterion being that the airline no longer blew out as many tires on landings. This was front-page news. But all this self-promoted national esteem had a Janus face to it, for meanwhile the government was silently scheming new insidious wheys to eradicate the Kurds, an item no paper dared print.

At the same time, Britain, was having its nose tweaked by something it, too, wanted to hide: Anthony Cavendish's MI-5 memoirs, material so sensitive that Her Majesty had **XXXXX**ed-out select passages.

It was subversive reading material that British subject, Dave Manby had smuggled into Turkey hidden in one of the kayaks on his van.

✦ ✦ ✦

The letter read: "My friend, I have very original trip to Turkey for you. Very old. Very cheap. For you, too, I give special price." Not only was it written on parchment but the r's were rolled. It was signed "Dave Manby."

◄ [Frank Cranbourne photo]

To participate I had to convince Frank, skipper of an Alaskan fishing boat on which I crew, that Turkey is a nice place to visit, so nice that he ought to cut the season short and join the trip . . . .

As we changed airports in New York the cab driver asked us, "Where are you going?"

"Turkey," we replied. "We've got to get there in the worst way."

He dropped us off at the YouGoSlave counter.

Our departure was a dismal scene. When they discovered what airlines their friends and relatives were flying, those left behind wept uncontrollably.

As we boarded the plane we noted that the stewardesses were **XXXXXXXXXXXX** and wearing **XXXXXXXXXXX**.

"Sit down!" one greeted me.

"I can't. There's a man sitting in my seat."

"Zat is no reason. Sit down and shut up."

"But . . ."

"If you don't stop zis complaining I vill take you in smelly Communist bathroom with happy music zat drags through tape deck and zere I vill teach you a thing or two, you non-Serburbian pig!"

"But there's a man in my seat!"

With this she **XXXXXXXXXXXXXX** and **XXXXXXXXXXXXXX XXXXXXX**, whips **XXX** chains.

"Zere! Zat vill teach you!" she said as she slipped back into her leather underwear. "Now zen!"

"There's *still* a man in my seat." I said. This time she **XXXXXXX XXXXXXXXXXXX**!!!**XXXXXX** and **XXXXXXXXXX XXXXXXXX XXXXX XXXX**.

Twelve hours later, while we were still awaiting clearance to taxi, two mechanics suddenly appeared on the wing. They stood on the part that says, "No Step," one holding a crescent wrench, the other a ball-peen hammer. The first took out a pocketknife and pried open a tiny little door, while the second mechanic began scratching his **XXXX**s. Peering in the opening they discussed a subject they were very concerned about—like football scores. One pointed at something while the other shrugged. Then they closed the door and began laughing. After a while we **XXXXXXXXXXXXXXXX**.

Somewhere over the Atlantic the captain came on to tell us he hated all Croats and Muslims that might be aboard and oxygen would only be given to Serburbanites in case of an emergency. When we landed in Belgrade at last, everyone applauded, an

indication that successful landings with this airline are not to be taken for granted.

In the airport I ran into a girl from my sixth-grade class (I'm not kidding!)—only now she was grown and dressed in black. It was wonderful to reminisce.

She said, "Do you remember John White?"

"Yes. What's he doing?"

"He died in a car crash. Remember Steve Wilson?"

"Oh, yeah, I remember him. How's he?"

"He died of AIDS. How about Mary McCulloch?"

"Yeah, what a sweetheart."

"She got killed in an avalanche! Do you remember . . . "

"Excuse me, I just heard my flight called. It was fantastic seeing you again. Believe me."

I found Frank. He said, "What the *XXXX* happened to you? You look like you've seen a ghost."

"Worst than that," I assured him.

"What are you doing?"

"Praying, and if you were smart you'd start too."

Miraculously, we reached Istanbul alive. But expecting our bags to arrive as well was akin to Oliver asking for seconds. Our gear had been sent to *XXXXXX* and if we didn't like it, the YouGo agent informed us, we could *XX XXXX* our *XXXXX*s.

Whoever designed Istanbul must also have designed London. There is no sense to it whatsoever. A map for one will *XXXX* on the other. It didn't take more than a few minutes to become hopelessly lost. Frank and I tried to find our way back to our hotel and became certain it had been torn down in our absence. At last we hired a taxi and offered the driver expensive gifts, eternal happiness, and a large financial reward if he could find it for us. He whipped a U-turn, drove half a block, turned left, and dropped us off at the front door.

Flying to Ankara we picked up several more members of the trip, among them Green Slime. Airborne once more, I pointed out the Euphrates.

"If that's the Euphrates," said a passenger who claimed to be a librarian, "then we are in Egypt."

Slime said, "Bloody hell! If we're in Egypt, then we're on the wrong plane." Then, while he was putting iodine in his coffee, he asked me, "Aren't librarians supposed to be the fountain of knowledge?"

"Don't know. I'm not a librarian."

I got up for more coffee but the stewardess took me in the bath *XXXXXXXXXXXXXXXXXXXXXXXXXXXXXXXXXXXXXXXXXX XXXXX XXXXXXXXXX XXXXX XXXXX*.

"Those really are wonderful carpets," I thanked her and returned to my seat.

In Erzurum we were met, not by Dave Manby, but by a friendly taxi driver; with Brylcream in his hair, hope in his eyes, and deception in his heart, he immediately befriended us. Charging us double his meter, he drove us to a carpet shop, run by his father—a relic older than auld lang syne—who greeted us heartily and told us that nothing was closer and dearer to his heart than his pacemaker.

"He's lying through his teeth!" Frank whispered.

"I don't think so," I said. "Looks like he's taken them out." He beckoned us to sit and plied us with tea, which Slime immediately annihilated with iodine. It was then that Dave Manby and Greystoke of N.O.C. (Natahala Outdoor Center) walked in. Slime spilt his tea on a very expensive white silk carpet.

"No problem," said Greystoke of N.O.C. (Not Our Carpets) and we piled into Dave's van.

Today, auto manufacturers canvas millions of people when they are designing vehicles. To demonstrate how effective this million-dollar research is, just imagine Dave buying his van.

Salesman: "So, you'd like a van."

Dave: "Yes."

Buddhist monk, Spiti, India

The Spiti, India

▲▲ On the road to the Euphrates, Turkey. ▲ Surfing the Euphrates. [Carol Haslett photo]

The Euphrates, Turkey. Note the springs. These lined the river for several miles.

▲▲ The Tortem, a tributary of the Choruh, Turkey. ▲ Bus station, Pokhara, Nepal.

The Marsyandi, Nepal.

▲▲ The Motu, New Zealand. ▲ The Gilza, Pakistan.

The Swat, Pakistan

The Landsborough, New Zealand.

Muddy Creek, Utah.

▲▲ Mardi Gras, New Orleans. ▲ The Toutle, Washington.

▲▲ Canyon wall at evening, the Grand Canyon. ▲ Carol and Granite Rapid, the Grand Canyon.

Mike Savory on the Kunhar, Pakistan. Believing he was spreading goodwill
the handshake actually secured him a wife and a flock of sheep.

Salesman: "How heavy?"
Dave: "Doesn't matter."
Salesman: "What size engine?"
Dave: "Doesn't matter."
Salesman: "Color?" (Actually the salesman said, "*colour?*")
Dave: "Doesn't matter."
Salesman: "Does *anything* matter?"
Dave: "Yes, it can't be more than six foot, three inches wide."
Salesman: "Why's that?"
Dave: "Because there's a certain bridge in eastern Turkey I've got to drive across."

As for the health of Dave's van's, the shocks were coming through the wheel wells, the length of welds added to the front end could be measured in yards, and most of the bolts that were holding together what was left of the vital parts had been persuaded into place permanently with a hammer. At a mechanic's school, the engine was a final exam for anyone going for a doctorate. In all, the van was worth about twenty-five dollars—providing it was filled with gas.

We spent the day in Erzurum, a place considered by the rest of Turkey to be a cold lonely outpost. It is as fundamentalist Muslim as Nebraska is Christian, and like Nebraska, the women dress in large gunnysacks that come in two color choices, brown or black.

Erzurum, considered to be a mild purgatory by the rest of Turkey. In winter, at the local ski area, wolves chase errant skiers back inbounds.

Junior Birdmen,
Muslim division.

These are wrapped over the head and cover the face, forcing the women inside to steer by radar.

Besides, it is not healthy for a Muslim woman to be seen by an infidel, a person like Frank, who has no rein whatsoever on his need-of-washing, lecherous western mind. Freely speculating what was—or wasn't—being worn *under* this garb, he exclaimed: "I see tassels! Butt floss bikinis! Sequins and lace! Silk Teddies! I've never been so **XXXXXX XX**!"

Often a kid or two clung to the sack. Our eroding culture is plagued with abandoned kids. But here a child who has come unclung merely latches onto the next passing gunny sack and never knows the difference since they've never actually seen their mother in the first place.

In the evening we walked up to the citadel overlooking the city and listened to the coyotes howling.

"You're an idiot!" Dave said, "Those aren't coyotes, those are muslim imams calling everyone to prayer."

"You mean I've just bought a ranch in Oregon surrounded by muslim imams?"

Yet despite the area being zealously Islam, the people are not at all what you might think. Unlike the Ayatollah Khomeini, who had his sense of humor surgically removed, these folk are always up for a laugh.

Heading for the Choruh river we stopped once for gas (and to look at carpets) and for lunch (where we looked at more carpets). Greystoke of N.O.C. (Not Our Car) drove over a large boulder and put a small gash in the oil pan. "No problem," he said and **XXXXXXXXXXX XXXXXXX XXXXXXXXXXXXXX**.

The geography we drove through couldn't decide whether it was mountains or hills. There was nothing jagged about it, yet it was steep and immense, with no fences and few cottages to give it perspective. It was grasslands that appeared to roll on forever, still green at July's end due to an above-average snowpack and an unseasonably wet summer.

We camped where we met the river, creek-like in appearance. Dave produced some Turkish Delight and a bottle of Russian vodka. Slime immediately put iodine in it.

One of the persons of our group demanded, "Where can I buy Turkish Delight in Turkey?"

"Same place you can buy Russian vodka in Russia," Dave replied.

The next day we floated to the village of Ispir, a section where river and land peacefully coexisted. Ispir was built on a hillside at the confluence of the Choruh and a large stream. Looking up this valley, I caught my first glimpse of big mountains in Turkey, serious threats to navigation for anyone who is piloting an ark.

That night at the hotel, Greystoke of N.O.C. (Not Our Culture) gave us instruction on how to squat on the toilets. Certainly no gender-spawned arguments have ever started in Turkey over putting the seat down. But that is not why I remember Ispir. I remember it for a shave—a close one, that Frank and I went for in the morning. Naïvely, we entered a barbershop only to be glared at by a *XXXXX* barber who was busy sharpening a straight-edge. He muttered something in Turkish that didn't sound nice.

"What did he say?" I wondered aloud.

"He said you're first," Frank said.

As the barber lathered my throat, Frank said, "Give me fifty bucks or I'll tell him you're a Christian."

"*XXXXXXXX* you!" I said from under the lather.

"He's going to shave your beard off for that."

"No, he's not."

Unfortunately, the barber, who had evidently studied under Lizzie Borden, was still not in a joking mood—and never had been in his whole life. With two quick swipes of his razor he erased my beard. Three more carves left me with a Camel-filter mustache, and if he'd insisted on any more I would have looked like a chicken neck in a packaged fryer. Getting into my kayak I was still wiping the shaving cream off my face.

Downstream from Ispir—and thanks to Ispir—the river's various levels were marked by trash snagged on the bank-side brush; the tamarisk looked like Christmas trees decorated by drunks. However, I didn't mind the garbage as much as I did the landscape. Here it was taking an immediate dislike to the river. There were rapids everywhere. I've never before been on a river and thought: "What would happen here in an earthquake?" And there were more rapids waiting to happen just a low Richter-rating away. The river increased in difficulty, and the drops, at last, required a good scout.[1] Somewhere along the way we were all swept over—according to a certain book by *XXXXXX XXXXX*—a 15-foot waterfall, unrunnable in any craft.

Downstream, we began to pass hundreds of castles. Well, a few anyway. Obviously, somebody, at some point in history, built a low-cost housing development of them. To get an idea of how old they were, I asked a local their age. Shrugging, he informed me that they were there when he was born.

In time we reached Yusufeli, a quaint little village where the

[1] Unfortunately, we didn't have one.

At a safer barbershop: Mustafa's in Yusufeli where each day I kept having more close shaves. This little shaver was the apprentice barber. [Dave Manby photo]

entire population seemed to be employed jackhammering the streets into rubble. It was here that one of our herd began reading the part in the guidebook about black plagues and all the instant, fatal diseases that can be had *just from smelling local water*. In no time at all we quickly **XXXXXXXX**ed ourselves by buying up the town's entire supply of bottled water. Only then did Dave point out—while Slime was filling his bottled water with iodine—that we were spending a great portion of our time upside-down in a river filled with raw sewage and sheep guts. But don't get the wrong idea about the sheep guts. If ever you came out of your boat and needed extra buoyancy, you were never more than an arm's length away from a stomach. It just wasn't wise to run out of breath close to shore where various other entrails had stewed and rotted.

We stayed in Yusufeli for five nights. The days were torturously hot when we were not on the water. In the evenings we sat on the balcony of a small bar overhanging the river, which pleasantly cooled the air. There, we sat listening to the chuckle of the river—and the plop of garbage being incessantly thrown into it. One night at the bar we discovered a thick red wine—that Slime put iodine in. However, the following day we awoke with our vision still blurred. "You've contacted retsina," the local optometrist informed us. "A horrible regional disease that makes you go blind."

Which didn't help us, for that day we were to run the biggest section of water. It was our sixth day and the river now tumbled with muscled velocity—at least that's what we thought until we arrived at two back-to-back drops that made everything upstream insignificant. The first **XXXX** was the hardest. Its entry was through three v's, the third flanked by a hole as friendly as a YouGoSlave stewardess. Next came a scramble right, a route requiring luck and hard punches through some gnarly breaking waves. Following this was an alluvial spread of river and boulders, easy to pick through in

The Tortem, a tributary of the Altu, which in turn is a tributary of the Choruh, which is . . . well never mind. Unlike the Choruh, this river contained very few sheep stomachs. Missing a roll left nothing to grab.

a boat but an unhealthy place for a swim. Several of the group still insisted upon doing so, and their kayaks were trashed in the process.

"No problem," said Greystoke of N.O.C. (Not Our Cayaks).

Although much of this drop was natural, some was not. Only the year before, Dave, about to enter the drop, was distracted by people on the bank yelling and waving frantically at him. "Friendly people," he thought, and waved back. Just then an explosion spewed an avalanche of boulders into the river in front of him. The hydroelectric people were testing the rock for a future dam that some day will **XXXX** the Choruh[2].

Finished with the Choruh, a handful of us commandeered Dave and his van to gallivant around Eastern Turkey in the manner of an old Jack Lemmon/Tony Curtis movie. We even cruised by Ararat—but a lot of good *that* did us with kayaks on the van (though you never know when a flood can happen). We meandered farther south and it was impossible to tell if we were looking for something or running away from returning to mundane lives. There were things, however, that we could never escape, like the effects of Dave's curry. We had become living cappuccino makers, all hisses and gurgles, followed by a permeating stench of long, agricultural farts. Another unavoidable object was the beady-eyed, bushy-eyebrowed, **XXXXXXX**, thin-lipped vampire stare of Ataturk.[3] His picture hung everywhere, even in public rest rooms. Such a pity; given a pair of fangs, he could have been truly infamous. And lastly were the carpet salesmen. The trip was not measured in days or miles, but in assaults by these arachnids who insisted they *weren't* carpet salesmen at all—but just happened to have several hundred carpets to pawn off anyway.

At last, we headed for the Euphrates, a river first run by **XXXXXX XXXXX**, the **XXXX**-known author, an incredible feat considering the Italians had run it twenty years earlier. Along the way we passed a broken-down VW, owned, no less, by Germans. "What's wrong?" Greystoke of N.O.C. (Not Our Conundrum) asked.

"Ve don't know."

"Well, if you're German and can't fix a VW then we sure can't help you," he informed them.

Our plan to run the Euphrates was a simple one. Parking the van at the take-out we would catch the train upstream, get off where we **XXXX** liked, then drift back to the van. We had already **XXXX**ed that day's train but the next **XXXXXX** was due at 4:00 the

---

[2] At least it will keep some of the garbage out of the Black Sea.

[3] As an alcoholic in a hard-line Muslim country he was often caught between arrack and a hard place.

following morning. I seriously doubted we'd be on it. If it was at 4:00 the following afternoon, maybe; but one we had to get up for, never.

We camped just outside the station and set the alarm for 3:00, which is exactly when it went off. But 3:00 is such a hostile hour, and since no one else in the vicinity was getting up we saw no reason to either. At 3:50, lying in the warmth of our bags, we could see, distantly, the train's light, but since the train was in no hurry to get to the station we didn't rush there either. At 3:55, however, the train was closer to the station than we were; we scrambled like ants evacuating a smoking log. But, of course, by the time we'd gathered our gear it was too late. We arrived on the platform as the train pulled away.

"Oh **XXXX**," said Greystoke of N.O.C. (Not Our Connection).

However, in countries like Turkey,[4] there is always regularity in the irregularity; on that particular day of that particular month, another train followed. However, despite having a two-hour warning, and our gear piled on the platform, we still barely made it.

We detrained at Kemah, once the capital of Kurdistan. Now it was just another sleepy Turkish village—or so it appeared, but bygones are not bygones. Three weeks later I hiked across the Munzer mountains, though I was warned against it because of bears, wolves, and Kurdish guerrillas. Of course, I figured it was just local paranoia; on my hike I saw none of the above. I arrived at Kemah in the morning and left. In the afternoon the guerrillas, materializing from the mountains, shot dead eight soldiers. It sure made me wonder about the bears and wolves.

As for the Euphrates, it was an easy river: mud-laden, and about as far away as you can get from carpet salesmen in Turkey. Shortly after Kemah, the river carves through a gorge that is filled with magnificent scenery—a setting I would have to drive, say, at least forty-five minutes from my home to find. The difference is that these cliffs issue thousands of springs that produce the freshest, purest water on earth—and Slime still put iodine in it. These cliffs had also been environmentally tampered with by the Romans. An ancient road had been carved along the gorge wall. In one place we came to a tiny rock fort with a tunnel extruding down to the river—no doubt to access water when the fort was under siege from attacking carpet salesmen.

The river, too, had a distinct Biblical feel to it. There were shepherds with flocks, snakes hanging out in apple trees, a skeleton

---

[4] One with trains.

from a Roman umpire, hillsides afire with burning bushes, men who looked like Charlton Heston—although some of the women might have, too, if they'd taken off their sacks—and certain places in the river where the entire group was in danger of being smitten. I was so moved that, for a while, I tried jotting notes in Biblical vernacular: "And David did sayeth: 'He's over and out' (10:4). And Slime looketh up and addeth: 'Don't bet on it,' (Horses 6 to 1). And later at thy dinner table, Greystoke of N.O.C. (Not Our Culinarian) did declare, 'What the *heck* is this???' (Diet of Worms 6:3). And after eating he did yelleth out frantically, 'Where's the (John?' 14:5) In the morning, Frank yelleth, 'Hey, there's a big hairy spider in my boat!' (Revelations 17:4). And the devil, he did command, 'GO TO *XXXX*!' Area code:(666). From the distance a chorus of voices rang out, 'We didn't build this place in a day!' (Romans 8:1) 'Hey!' (Jude 5:3)."

In time we came to a perfect little surfing wave, our idea of Eden, and we camped. Walking around I expected to see lewd Eden hieroglyphics depicting men and women with their clothes on but there was none of that. Temptation arrived the next morning and came in the form of two sixteen-year-old girls who appeared out of

Carol, surfing the Euphrates, about to swallow a large portion of history.

nowhere. Frank, blissfully joking—and never one to resist tempta-tion—addressed the first, and asked, "Will you marry me? If it's yes, answer me with silence."

Neither girl said a thing. We gave them some chocolate. Then they left. We picked up camp, floated downstream and, late in the day, camped once more. At dusk the two girls made another unex-pected appearance in camp and, speaking excitedly in Turkish, informed us that they were running away to America with us.

"There you go, Frank," I said.

"And a wife for you, too, Dave," Slime added.

"But I don't live in America," Dave protested.

"Boy, will *she* be disappointed then," Slime said.

"Shouldn't have kidded around, Frank," I added.

"But they didn't understand a word I said!"

"Few women do."

"Seriously, what we do?"

"Who's we? Don't stand there, say you'll marry one of them."

One of the girls spoke.

"They say their fathers beat them," Dave translated.

"Tell them that's OK, you won't beat them," Slime advised.

Since it was too dark for them to return to their village, we put them with Dave's sister for the night. In the morning, after Dave, once more, painstakingly explained to the girls that it just wouldn't work out, we bid them what we hoped was a permanent goodbye and they left. We looked around and enjoyed the scenery one last time—for about fifteen seconds—stuffed our gear into our boats pell-mell, and quickly sprinted downriver for our take-out, before the girls decided to follow us any further.

◆　◆　◆

Several days later I was on my own, standing under the eave of a building waiting for a rain squall to pass. Quickly I was joined by a man who spoke English, an old woman, and a gang of accredited urchins who pointed at me and began laughing hysterically. The man said, "They are laughing at you."

I said nothing.

The woman scolded them, but it did no good. The man again spoke the obvious. He said, "She told them to stop, that they have no manners."

Dave Manby being
unmercifully attacked by
his conscience.

Again the woman admonished them but this time in cold terse language. Instantly the kids were rendered shocked, quiet, and somber.

I asked, "What did she tell them *that* time?"

He replied, "She said the same God that made you made them."

The little **XXXXXX**s.

RESCUE

On the Low Seas

I was informed by the captain of a trader, a trustworthy person, that he once approached the island to trade, in rough weather, but could not send a boat ashore, as it was impossible to land. He lay as close as he dared under the lee of the island. Here they saw the Innuit tying several men securely into their kyaks, on the top of the rock, some fifteen or twenty feet above the water. When all was done each man grasped his double-ended paddle, and two others took the kyak by bow and stern and tossed it, with its occupant, into the water. For a moment they disappeared under the waves, but instantly rose and righted themselves; in a few minutes they were alongside, and being taken on board, produced furs and ivory from their kyaks, with which they proceeded to trade for tobacco and other articles.

—William H. Dall, *Alaska and its Resources*, 1870

◆ ◆ ◆

Over the years I've watched sea kayaking, like river kayaking, be consumed by consumerism. Only more so. For boat manufacturers, retailers, (and a healthy GNP), sea kayaking has become an insatiable, gouge-sized niche for wannabe yacht owners. Boats are now adorned with more gadgetry than in a Dick Tracy cartoon. There are rudder housings and bilge pumps and global positioning systems and auxiliary stirrups and signal flares and enough bulkheads to keep a kayak afloat after—should the navigating systems fail—collisions with various bigger-than-bread-box objects. In short, today's cars come with fewer options than sea kayaks. A person buying a sea kayak might ask, "Yes, but do I really *need* all those doodads?"

And the salesman will subtly imply: "No, absolutely not. But don't let anyone catch you calling yourself a sea kayaker if you don't have all the goodies."

This was all brought home to me recently when I was out paddling and ran into a group of this new breed of boater on a beach on Vancouver Island's west coast. As they approached and began to scrutinize me, I immediately felt like a lesser being, since my clothing bore no stickers and my gear had no labels. They, on the other hand, began taking various stances that allowed me to read at least seven logos on each one of them. I glanced at their gear: It was plastered with manufacturers' names so large that even the passengers in jetliners traveling overhead could discern the letters. At last, after saying hello, one of them inquired, "How did you make it here alive without stickers all over your equipment?"

I shrugged modestly and admitted I didn't rightly know. After that I thought the tone of things might deteriorate, that perhaps for all the money they had spent on equipment, I, intruding on *their* remote beach, might be staining their truly unique wilderness experience. But I was mistaken. Instead, I was just what was lacking. To assure themselves that they were sea kayakers of a high caliber, they needed an audience. For the next millennium I listened patiently as they expounded on their sea-faring accomplishments. They talked freely of drogues, of surf capabilities,[1] of night navigating, of sniffing out land when it disappears from sight, of seal launches from breaker-washed rocks into gale-tossed seas, of sleeping comfortably in a kelp bed, and on and on until my jaw hinge developed tendinitis from yawning. I could see there was no end to their exploits, that if I politely continued to listen to them, we would all be there until winter. I tried to interrupt by saying I had to go, but this was to no avail. They kept on until I was forced to use more drastic measures. Fortunately, I discovered their achilles heel: The most coveted merit badge was missing from their repertoire. In a nano-second lull I wedged in my question,

[1] Not wishing to show my ignorance I didn't ask what this was, whether this was equipment or a technique. However, since that time I have decided it is both. Surf capability means that any survivors should have with them a waterproof cell-phone to call 911, suture equipment, splints for multiple fractures, and large doses of pain killers.

"Has any one of you ever been involved in a sea rescue?"

There was complete silence.

"No? You mean to tell me you all call yourselves sea kayakers and not one of you has ever taken part in such a rescue?"

They dropped their heads in embarrassment.

"Well, let me tell you," I said, as I thumped my chest. "I *was* involved in one, and it was no simple matter either."

"What happened?" one asked, gazing at me with sudden reverence.

"For starters, it hardly went according to the textbook, though admittedly I've never read one on the subject."

"Bad weather?" another asked hopefully, his curiosity overcoming his chagrin.

"Nope. It was flat calm. There were three of us out paddling: my girlfriend, a guy called Greystoke, and myself. We came across the victim swimming."

"The victim wasn't in your party?"

"No, she was about a mile from shore, rather confused and turning hypothermic. All by herself."

"Incredible. Where was her kayak?"

"Didn't have one, not that I could see. Didn't even have on a life jacket."

"No life jacket!"

"Heck! *She wasn't even wearing clothes!*"

"You must be kidding!"

"I'm not. All she wore was a startled look on her face. We tried talking to her but it did no good. She began to panic and tried climbing up on our boats, which got the three of us arguing over logistics. I thought it best to tie her up but my girlfriend wanted to know how I'd feel if she fell back in. Greystoke said not to worry, that he'd had a lot of experience with sheep . . . "

"What sort of experience?"

"He didn't say, but he did suggest sitting the victim in his lap. He said that had a soothing effect."

"On whom?"

"He didn't say that either. Will you let me continue? Thank you. We went with Greystoke's proposal and, rafting up, we wrestled the victim aboard, stuffing her into Greystoke's cockpit. She wasn't too happy about it either but in time she calmed down."

"Did she talk then?"

"Nope."

RESCUE

"We took her to shore and I'll tell you: By now she was *really* hypothermic. Fortunately, though, our fire was still going so we pushed sand over the coals and put her on top."

"You didn't climb in a sleeping bag with her?"

"No. I was worried she might have lice but the warm sand did the trick. She recovered quickly—which was too bad in a way."

"What do you mean, "too bad!' *You didn't care if she lived?*"

I shrugged. "Oh, I was happy to see her make it. But on the other hand, I do like venison."

Greystoke carrying out the rescue. We had paddled into this bay looking for whales.

UTAH

When You Say "Mud" You've Said it All

On rapids keep to the mainstream, or else you might get caught in backwaters.

—Col. Narendra Kumar, *Indus Boat Expedition*, 1978

◆　◆　◆

I was born independently lazy. What has befallen me since has been no idea of my own, but rather other people's conniving schemes. Take how I came to run Muddy Creek. Making a short story long, it began one January, years ago, when Carol drove me to the North Rim of the Grand Canyon, just above Lava Falls. There the road ends—no warning signs, nothing; just a cliff a car could go right over, which I suggested to Carol would be the best way to fix the exhaust leak in her Volkswagen. She would have none of this. (Sometimes women can be so disagreeable.) Quickly, we were met by the ranger—but not the ranger Carol had brought me out to meet. "What happened to him?" Carol asked.

"He's buried right over there."

The replacement said he was only temporary, "Filling in," he explained and nodding his head once more towards the grave added, "Like he's doing." The replacement said he had always wanted isolation but didn't mean for his prayers to be answered so thoroughly: We were the first people he'd seen in a month. He was so starved for company that when I dragged out the tent he said, "Put that away and come back to the hut. It's going to snow tonight."

In the warmth of his hut the ranger spoke of his two sources of entertainment. One was chipping arrowheads from pop bottles. In the summer he sprinkled these around signs warning that it was an offense to

◀ Bill walking (as opposed to running) a drop on the Muddy. Leash laws are extremely tough in Utah.

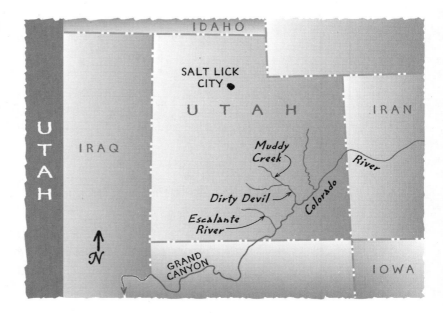

take artifacts. His other amusement was an on-going feud with weather statisticians—"bureaucratic imbeciles," he called them—people whose lives centered solely on data. In his monthly reports he would either send in dates without precipitation or vice versa, but never complete figures.

He was so adamantly opposed to paperwork that later, when I requested a hiking permit, he told me not to worry about one. He advised us, "If you want to see more desert, go hike Coyote Wash up by Escalante."

So we did.

Afterwards, looking at my pictures of this hennaed landscape, it seems like it is a real pretty place, but with January's snowstorms and freezing weather, it didn't give me that impression at the time. (Later in the season this hike has the largest ratio of Sierra Clubbers to scared-off wildlife of anywhere in the country.)

At the end of Coyote Wash there was an arch which people spoke of as if it were the end of the yellow brick road, the pot of gold under the rainbow, and the winning lotto numbers all rolled into one. But really it is a defective slab of rock with a hole in it. What did attract my attention was the Escalante river flowing under it and I asked myself: What the heck am I doing hiking here when I could have floated to this very spot?

The next year, Carol and I returned with our kayaks and ran the river. But running the shuttle was harder. I had a muffler-less (it fell off), license-less (never had one) motorcycle in the back of my truck. When a local asked what I was planning to do, he told me not to let the sheriff catch me on the roads. Then he informed me that on Sundays—the very next day—the sheriff would be in church from 10:00 to 11:00. Then he proceeded to tell me about someone the month before whose jeep had just been found wrecked, off road. "The guy," he said, "was burnt half up."

"What happened to the other half?"

"The coyotes et it."

After eluding both the sheriff and coyotes, we spent seven days on the river and, intending to write an article on it, I jotted down:

✍ Find out what an Escalante is and what sort of
  sauce goes best on one.
✍ Find out if the people who ran this before us wrote
  anything about it and, if not, claim a first.
✍ Find out name of that arch and if nameless,
  name it after self.

We enjoyed the Escalante so much we returned the following year to run another Colorado river drainage north of the Escalante. This river, the Dirty Devil, was so filled with mud and alkali that we had to carry a ten day's supply of water—although twenty days of beer would have worked just as well.

This time, with the renewed intention of adding to my article, I had read up on the Dirty Devil. Jack Sumner, a member of Major Powell's trip, compared this river to the sewer of Sodom and Gomorrah. I was sorry that I had ever checked. (And what was Sumner doing in the Sodom and Gomorrah sewer anyway?) Powell claims he said it was a "dirty devil" and named it such, but another account claims that Powell named it after one of the Howland brothers, for at this point tensions were running high in the trip (Powell's trip, not ours; we still had alcohol). This, too, makes me wonder about the weight of such insults and I imagined the fight they must have had:

"Dumb-dumb."

"Stupid."

"Oh yeah. Well you're a rat!"

"Goat!"

"Goat? PIG!"

"PIG? Why you're a JACKASS!"

"What! Call me a JACKASS! HHHH! How dare you, why you're a . . . you're a *DIRTY DEVIL!*"

It reminded me of the third grade, when Gene Allison called

the teacher a *butt*. He was marched off to the principal's office and we all merrily speculated that if he was sentenced to die in the electric chair, he was getting off easy. But times have changed. Today he would have shot *her*. My point is, however, is this: If halfway down the Colorado, Powell and Co. were calling each other dirty devils, then to what level did the name-calling escalate

More Muddy Creek.

by the trip's end? *What did* Powell call the Howland brothers and Dunn to insult them enough to leave?

The first camp (Carol's and mine, not Powell's) we stayed at the draw leading up to Robber's Roost. The next day we set out to hike up the draw to the Roost, anxious to see a spot of American history. I mean, England knows where the Magna Carta was signed; America has Robber's Roost. So you can understand our building anticipation as we hiked toward a natural corral fouled by Butch Cassidy's and the Sundance Kid's stolen horses. But after a mile or so we tired of hiking in the sun, and I said to Carol, "Isn't it amazing to be in a draw that Butch Cassidy and The Sundance Kid probably rode down?"

She agreed and we turned around.

I made notes for my article:

✎ Which one did Redford play and which one did
   Newman play?
✎ If this is the desert, why did B. J. Thomas keep singing
   Raindrops keep falling on my head?
✎ What does B. J. really stand for?

That was the last entry in my journal. Over the next nine days I know *something* happened but I'm not sure what. I'm sure we made it to the end successfully because we each said what a good trip it was and how we'd come back and do another like it. I know we said this because several years later we were back, kayaks on car, looking for Muddy Creek, a tributary of the Dirty Devil that crosses the San Rafeal Swell.

Notes:

✎ Find out who Muddy was. Also San Rafael.
   Did he like Escalantes and what did he put on them?
✎ What made San Rafael swell?
✎ Why didn't anyone ever shoot B. J. Thomas?

We crossed several dry gulches, but no Muddy Creek. Thinking the map in error we continued on but still arrived at no creek. So we took a side road to a side town, and sidling up to one of the locals asked, "OK, whaddid you do with Muddy Creek?"

"You crossed it just back there."

"No we didn't."

"Yes, you did, two miles back."

"*That* was it! You call *that* a creek!"

"We do when there's water in it. Say, you weren't planning on running it were you, with them there kieyaks?"

"What, *us*? Ha, you must be joking! That's a good one! No, ah, we were on our way to the Colorado!"

It was hard believing we'd driven all that way to run a creek with the drainage area the fetch of the New York sewer system—and it was waterless. After that, we kept tabs on each year's snowpack. Only five years later was there enough snow to melt for a run off, which, as we discovered, was still inadequate. This time, "we" equaled four as Carol and I alone did not wish to appear so stupid. We had talked some friends, Bill and Gerri, into coming, insisting that this would be far cheaper than a vacation in Europe.

There was enough water to float our boats, though not enough if we sat in them. But this was not a problem, we reasoned. Surely the creek would pick up water down stream.

It didn't. And within a day we were lost. It's hard to believe, but right off the bat, using a wrong draw as a reference point, we identified all other draws downstream to fit our perception of how the land should correspond to the map. It hardly mattered. We had two weeks worth of food but, in retrospect, if we'd thrown it away perhaps our boats would have had enough draw for us to sit in.

Here it is best to refer to the notes:

DAY 1: Small holes in boats. Wish we'd brought small repair kit.

DAY 2: Bill's waterproof camera bag, with camera, fills with water. Small holes in boat slightly bigger. Wish we'd brought slightly bigger repair kit.

DAY 3: Last night Bill tripped and fell on his $400 tent, breaking poles and ripping tent. Slightly bigger small holes getting larger in boats. I also fell and cut my arm. Bill, a vet, sewed my arm back together.

DAY 4: Holes now medium size. Wish we'd brought medium-sized repair kit. My arm seemed to heal but a strange urge to keep licking my wound came over me.

DAY 5: Bill lost his wife. Helicopter hovered over us and landed. Although we'd been lost all this time, the pilot said it took just forty-five minutes to find us. Pilot informed Bill he just lost his mother-in-law. Gerri flew off. Medium holes slightly larger. Wish we'd brought slightly larger repair kit.

DAY 6: Gerri's boat sank. We abandoned it. Bill said vacation in Europe would have been cheaper after all. Large holes in boats. Wish we'd brought a large repair kit. My arm is much better but now I have a bad case of fleas.

DAY 7: Large holes in boats growing larger and now only a 55-gallon drum of resin and roll of fiberglass can help them. I commented that perhaps it wasn't a good idea to bring fiberglass boats on the trip and Bill said, "You're right. Wheelbarrows would have worked much better. We could have floated through the pools and pushed them the rest of the way."

Bill walking out with the San Rafael Swell in the background. After ruining our boats, we wondered what was so swell about it.

Carol and Bill throw sticks in the river for me to fetch.
DAY 8: All boats sink. After we pile gear in large heap, Bill patted
    me on the head and said, "Good boy, go fetch the car."

Getting the car to our revised take-out was cause for worry
since the map showed the road as four-wheel drive only. However,
it is here that I shall put in a good word for drug-running. That
winter the smugglers (led by an ex-drug enforcement agent) bulldozed and leveled the road into a hidden runway just above our
new take-out. It's now the best road in the county. Unfortunately,
the drug-runners weren't aware that they should have landed their
plane between 10:00 and 11:00 on a Sunday when the sheriff was
in church. They were caught.

PAKISTAN

A Short Jeep Ride in the Hindu Kush

*My reception by the natives was generally civil, often humorous,
and sometimes exciting, when the boys who cheered the coming
stranger flung sods and mud up on him for a parting salute as he
retired from the bank.*

—John MacGregor, *The Rob Roy on the Jordan*, 1870

❖ ❖ ❖

Years ago, from a whitewater catalog, I ordered an item so insignificant
it isn't even logged in my memory. This mail-order company, with an
audacious leap of imagination, assumed that I was a rafter and sequentially
sold my name and address to several rafting mail-order outfits, which,
although I bought nothing from them, still pawned off my name to every
outdoor catalog on earth. These dweebs subsequently diversified my supposed interests: I became a gun-infatuated survivalist; I longed for CDs of
every imaginable genre of music; I collected cast hand-painted Civil War
soldiers. Then my sex was changed so I could crave diamonds and wear
lingerie (at least I *assumed* they had changed my sex) and so on until I
had to put in an industrial-sized mailbox just to accommodate this trash.
But I got tired of digging through this paper avalanche just to find my
bills, so I began a campaign. In the return, stamped envelopes into which
I was supposed to merrily deposit my checking account, I instead stuffed
rat droppings. I added the following advice: "The enclosed feces are from
laboratory rats that may have been used in experiments involving a
number of highly contagious fatal diseases. When you are through washing your hands, please delete my name from your mailing list."

The effect was immediate, and just when it looked like a junk-mail drought was setting in, a deadly new strain struck. It came in the form of a personalized letter—one that concerned a whitewater trip in Pakistan. It didn't even ask if I wished to participate but assumed I was already coming. Talk about a leap of imagination. The letter ended with, "I've got the boats lined up. Bring a paddle and gear. See you in Pindi, Sept. 21." It was signed Green Slime. There was no sending *him* rat turds, for not only was there no return envelope there was also no return address. He said he was in Nepal and couldn't be reached.

So . . . I was soon sitting in the Karachi[1] airport awaiting both my flight to Pindi and a chow mein I'd ordered. Although my flight would not leave for two hours, it was looking as though it would beat the chow mein. The restaurant's fluorescent lighting was just bright enough to highlight the grease on the floor, but not so bright that the rat ambling next to the wall was nervous. As I watched the rat slip into the kitchen I wondered if they had junk mail in Pakistan. There was a sudden flurry of activity in the kitchen and soon I had my plate of chow mein. Not that I'm saying it was *rat* chow mein, it's just that I would have digested the meal more easily had I also seen the rat exit the kitchen.

I don't know what it is about me that seems to attract the kind of people who sit next to me on airplanes. That is unless the maxim—"we are what we eat"—is true and if indeed the chow mein I'd just eaten had had a rat in it. I'd much rather have a philosophical discussion with my fellow passenger, say, "Do you think an anti-abortionist would abort an embryo if the embryo would grow into an abortion doctor?" Or, "How much should the Coriolis effect be factored in for spiraling inflation?" But no, on the PIA (Poor Inflight Alcohol) flight to Pindi, the fellow who sat next to me had a look in his eye that contained the shiftiness of a car peddler, the sleaze of an insurance huckster, and the pushiness of a realtor. And that was just in *one* eye. I won't even describe the fraud I saw brewing in the other. He said, "What do you do for a living?"

"I sell manure spreaders. I won't stand behind them though."

"I see. That is very interesting. Where are you from?"

"London."

"Ah, nice place, London. You must be a very rich man."

These leaps of imagination people kept taking with me! They

---

[1] Karachi, Sind. The British once took this province just so the C.O. could cable home, "I have Sind."

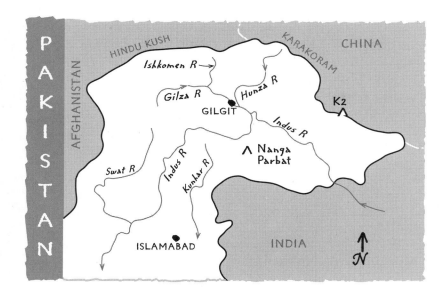

were beginning to set distance records. "What makes you think so?" I asked.

"You're flying."

"You're on the same plane."

"But I only come from Karachi."

"You should have taken the bus and saved some money then."

"I think you are a very smart person also."

Another world record! He went on to tell me of his own genius, but what a liability it was being so smart in a country so poor. And, as one genius to another, he asked, "What is your name?"

"Peter Knowles, although you can call me Slime."

"Mister Slime, I am very glad to meet you. I think we should go into business together. We will open the first McDonald's in Pakistan. I have seen them in London. The people who own them are very wealthy. But, there is a problem."

"What's that?"

"I need you to supply me with the money."

"What! And you contribute nothing!"

"Oh no, Mister Slime, I would have a much more difficult problem." I thought this might have something to do with pawning off bacon burgers, or keeping the McRats out of the Big Macs, but no, it was insuring that the cattle were slaughtered in the correct ceremonial Muslim manner. "The customers will get extremely upset if they find out the animals have been killed otherwise. They may start a riot." I agreed that that was a hell of a responsibility and I wondered how I'd explain the fallen arches to my banker. I shook my head sadly and said the deal was off. The McVisionary shrugged and said, "Maybe you will reconsider Mister Slime. Please let me have your address and I will write you."

"Sure," I said and gave him Slime's London address. "I can't wait to hear from you, in fact; I wait with bated halitosis."

In the shuffle to pick up bags I managed to lose the McVisionary and hooked up with a Pindi local who wanted to share a cab with me, and sell me on the city as well. He said, "We have clean air in Pindi because we have so few cars. Wait until you breathe the air! Clean!"

But dust hung as thick as fog in the air and the taxi's headlights plying through it rendered an eerie sense, as though the city had just been bombed. The man said nothing. I arrived at our pre-scribed hotel at 5:00 in the morning. Sitting out in front was a Canadian, Diesel Dave Coles,[2] a clearing house of jokes that were most likely illegal in Pakistan. While telling them, we watched the sun rise, and when it had muscled its way through the dust we found and woke up Slime and Marcus Bailie, an Irish spy and dis-tant relation to the Bailey Bridge. Slime, awaiting other trip members, stayed in Pindi, while Dave, Marcus, and I caught a PIA (Perhaps I'll Arrive) flight to Gilgit.

The air in Gilgit was just the way my taxi mate had wanted it to be in Pindi: clean, clear, and cancer-inducing—at least for males. The women in purdah—the ultimate sun block—had no worries. Gilgit's setting was the largest rock quarry I'd ever seen; it was a trundler's paradise, a pet rock sanctuary, and Sisyphus's worst nightmare all bundled into one. The cattle reflected this poor range; they were so skinny that their hides, stretching across their soup-bone frames, looked pre-tanned. The goats, though, were sur-viving adequately—at least those that weren't having their throats slit by the river's edge.

Picking up our boats, Dave, Marcus, and I immediately set off down the Gilgit River. We all agreed it was an easy float—for the first hundred yards. After that we felt like fought-over kids in a messy divorce between a tidal wave and a hurricane. And condi-tions worsened when we were involuntarily swept out more than five feet from the right bank of the river. We still have no idea

---

[2] Born July 14, 1955. Drowned January 29, 1995. Once, after touring Europe in an old junk car he drove it to Heathrow to catch his flight home. Parking it on the mezzanine a policeman duly informed him that his car would be towed away. "Don't bother," he answered. "I left the keys in it."

what the run of this river is like along the left bank; however, Diesel says he did see it. Occasionally we stopped for Marcus to take a picture of a bridge.

At the confluence of the Hunza and the Gilgit we were met with a sand-and-trash-laden wind so harassing we had to temporarily pull out. The sky was shredded, the river was tumbling boulders, and the clay cliff we stood under loosened pebbles on us. Diesel nodded towards a nearby village and said, "Whaddya say we go over and watch the veils blow off the women's faces?"

The Hunza was thick, gray, and churning, and when at last we put back on, I said to myself, "next time I come here I'll go practice first in the back of a cement truck." A clever comparison I thought, until I looked up "Hunza" in my Oxford Urdu Dictionary (O.U.D. not to be confused with the I.U.D.). Translated, it means, "The slosh in the back of a cement truck."

The Hunza frightened us so much that we went up and ran more of it the following day. Still, I can't claim to have boated it. I merely avoided catastrophe, working back and forth in the current next to the bank. I'd never seen such big holes.

"You remember Whit Deschner?"

"Yes."

"It's really too bad. He accidentally fell into a hole on the Hunza, and, well, yes, he did eventually wash out but he's never been able to complete a sentence since . . . ."

That sort of hole. Certainly not the place to find the longevity that the Hunza Valley is (thanks to blowhard, Lowell Thomas) erroneously noted for.

In time, the rest of the group arrived in Gilgit, Green Slime leading as usual from the back, claiming that there has never been a retreat he has been unable to lead. I won't mention any names, but the police register listed our group's occupations as the following: astronaut, indoor yacht instructor, necrophilic, prime minister, suicide bomber, and pile driver. I also noticed in the same register that a Dave Manby had been here several months before us. This Dave Manby however was a poll tax evader. Coincidence, but a paltry one, considering all the Manbys in England—you know, sort of like all the Shakespeares who wrote plays in the late 1500s.

Early the next morning, we grossly overloaded (two words in Urdu that have never before been coupled) the jeeps and headed up the Gilgit River on an incredible, paved, two-lane highway that

Members of the pro-Western corrupting faction—Green Slime, Fiona Cowie, Phil McClintock, Diesel Dave, and Mike Savory—after hitting a speed bump.

gave way fifty feet out of town into something our driver claimed was a road (but I don't think the goats using it believed him). The life expectancy of a jeep driver in Pakistan is about seventeen minutes. I have no complaints about the vehicle's air conditioning. The stereo system seemed a bit unbalanced, but this could have been because I spent most of my time hiking out the left side to keep us from turning over. The engine, however, ran worse than a badly tuned lawn mower, and, come to think of it, I push my mower less. We stopped to take numerous pictures, with Marcus snapping shots of bridges, and after a short while—sixteen hours—we arrived at camp. The dust we had been breathing all day had also settled in geologic layers in our hair and on our faces, giving everyone the appearance of instant aging—which is exactly how we felt. Old and grumpy.

Driving up we had paid little attention to the river's difficulty because, 1) during daylight it was too scary to look at, 2) at night we couldn't see it, and 3) it didn't matter because Dave Manby had given us his detailed written account of the run.

In the morning I awoke to the sounds of yaks and goats outside my tent. There were also people sounds I couldn't understand, followed by ones I could, like: "What the hell are they staring at?"

Answered by: "If a UFO landed on your front lawn wouldn't you bloody well watch it?"

"I suppose."

"And I'd charge 'em a couple hundred quid for landing rights, too."

At which point some broken English began demanding a couple of hundred rupees.

Peering out from my tent I saw some blue eyes and red heads in the crowd (ones that hadn't come with us), evidence that Alexander the Great got to someone's great-great-grandmom when he came through here. Who gave the Kashmiri goats their golden eyes is a matter of debate.

We piled again into the jeeps and drove to the top—12,250 feet—of Shandur Pass which harbors the closest polo grounds to the moon; not only a place where a polo player can die of pulmonary edema but where a mountain climber can be killed by an errant polo ball. Having reached this spot for no apparent reason at all, we turned around, drove two hours back to where we'd just come from, and, in the afternoon, as the sun began to abandon us, we put in on the Gilza, which was merely the upper reaches of the Gilgit.

Practicing in Gilgit for the polo Super Bowl at Shandur Pass. [Lefty Wright photo]

At four sharp each afternoon our drivers milked the jeeps for their ghee.

At first the valley was comparatively wide, a place that seemed to get little reprieve from winter. It reminded me of a tundra river snaking harmlessly through scrub willow, the valley's only trees. Beyond were over-grazed grasses, which dwindled and quickly succumbed to rock on the surrounding mountains. The mountains were lackluster grays and browns except for the occasional telltale mineral colors staining their flanks. Tiny islands of green betrayed springs, but they were all too few in a sea of rocks. The springs were meticulously channeled toward the small pockets of tillable soil, which seemed inadequate to account for and support the number of people who materialized from this vast rockscape to stare at us.

With more abruptness than the local government officials, the mountains closed in on the valley and the river started falling. I am still unsure whether the drops were all safely readable from the river as we eddy-hopped through them or if it was the invading cold that made it necessary to reach our take-out quickly before hypothermia took us out.

The following morning, skipping a steep canyon, we joined the indisputable Gilgit. After paddling for several hours, we crossed a lake. We viewed the place where the river issued from the lake with suspicion, for it held all the necessary ingredients for a catastrophe: a narrowing gorge with a vanishing point somewhere below the horizon. A row of poplars flanking the river diminished quickly to tops, then nothing. I hoped that the distant trees were merely stunted but my hope was quickly exterminated by the unwelcome sound of agitated water. Kids sprinted along the banks with determined purpose for they didn't want to miss telling their grandkids what befell the idiots in kayaks who once disappeared here.

To our jeep drivers who were following us downstream, it was all very funny. As we had paddled past them on the lake, they'd indicated that we were on a collision course with disaster. Two hours later we paddled back up the lake to where they were still waiting.

After our jeep-portage, the river continued to be consistently inconsistent. At least now we had the comforting knowledge that from here on down Dave had run the river, and in our possession was his detailed account. However, turning to it for the first time, we discovered that his advice was written on a single sheet of paper, and that it revealed two unexplained numbers, a "2" and, a "5." Considerable discussion ensued as to the numbers interpretation of these. Someone said the river must be a class 2 except for the 5s. Someone else claimed that the class 5 would take 2 hours to portage. Another thought that there were 2 class 5s. Or that there were 5 hours of class 2. And I said that if you multiply 2 times 5 and divide it by the number of members in the party, add to this all the loose change in everybody's pockets, and multiply this by the amount of beers in Pakistan, you'll arrive at the average I.Q. of the group. My point of view, however, was discounted as being sarcastic.

At times the river calmed enough for us to take note of the jagged scenery, but these stretches were not a place we could relax since we knew the river was storing up for some doozy of a drop, like the one where Kiwi Mike Savory got churned in an unsympathetic hole, a Popeye-fight-looking encounter.

Several days downstream, we took a side trip on the unrun Ishkoman, which had probably been overlooked by boaters because of the deceptively flat valley it runs through. The upper section had significant gradient but the water was channeled through gravel and the rapids were of little consequence. However, on the lower portion, the gravel turned into boulders and the water turned into classic rapids. Any more boulders, though, and the rapids would have turned us into classic disasters.

Slime "standing" in the
middle of the Ishkoman—
and on the dividing line
between the Hindu Kush
and the Karakoram.
[Corporal Tunnel photo]

The Ishkoman supposedly divides the Hindu Kush from the Karakorams, a major responsibility. This is as profound as saying, everything on the right bank is west of here and everything on the left bank is east of here. I stood there trying to distinguish the two ranges but all I saw were cadences of mountains and none looked any different from the others. Yet it's the species of stuff geologists fill large portions of their rock brains with—a harmless academic argument. Not like the fools who went and put a time zone right down the middle of Hell's Canyon on the Snake River so that every time you ferry you have to change your watch.

Back on the Gilgit the days blended together, and distances were only marked by obscure incidents, like the time we stopped near where the English explorer, George Hayward, was murdered. Searching my notes to give some depth to this account, I have: "Near alleged site, we ordered tea and chapatis. Would have set a new Guiness record of 560 cups of tea and 437 chapatis in ten min- utes, but unfortunately it was discovered that one of the group was on steroids and we were stripped of our award. Never did learn why they murdered George . . . ."

Farther down, one of the local landowners pulled us over and invited us to his garden for tea—which might have been the circum- stance that led to George's demise. Sitting on Persian rugs under apricot trees he spoke tenderly of his father and four mothers. Searching for conversation, I asked him how his father was.

"Dead," he replied. Good diplomacy told me not to bring up his mothers, which I'll bet five bucks is the very thing George went and commented on.

On the next-to-last day on the Gilgit, I specifically remember one drop. Slime and I took a jeep downstream to scout a section containing four rapids. We could see three of the drops, but not the fourth. However, since it resided in the middle of such user-friendly water, we didn't think it worth worrying over. Returning, we informed the group all the drops were OK.

Our unchecked rapid was the worst massacre of the trip. Someone entered to the right of me only to be skyrocketed and deposited upside down. To my left I saw the tip of a paddle waving like a surrender flag, its owner buried hopelessly in a large hole but trying to dig himself out. Taking the average of these two prevail- ing disasters I ran center into stair-stepping reversals and it was through no skill of my own that I was spit out upright.

After the Gilgit, we jeeped down the Hunza to the Indus to where I've never seen a more hideous section of whitewater. My mind's-eye kayaker met a swift death in every rapid. At the turn of the last century Sir Francis Younghusband had written of this section: " . . . so tremendous is its power it is almost terrifying to watch." But having never seen it from a thousand feet up in an overloaded jeep threatening to tip over and join the river at each corner, Francis could hardly have known the true meaning of "terrifying."

Besides being stopped by soldiers because Marcus was taking pictures of bridges (and nearly had to sacrifice his film) we were also stopped at Chilas, where the police demanded bribes; they were old race jockeys who liked doing a little business on the side. ("Please let us pass. Come on! We'll give you a cookie!") With the building of the Karakoram Highway in 1974, the police and their "protection" had arrived. Although the highway killed all hope of an independent Kashmir, the widespread bribery and robbery has brought great economic gain to the region.

Next, came the Swat, a river beckoning us from Wick Walker's guide. Rumor has it that Wick wrote his book[3] while working at the U.S. embassy, and since then every boater who passes through Pakistan calls the embassy.

I can just imagine the conversation with his boss:

"Wick!"

"Yes, sir?"

"We're here in Pakistan trying to run clandestine, top-secret, covert operations and we've had to put on two new operators just to handle your friends calling you."

"They're not my friends, sir."

"And this mob outside our gate! Their jeeps are loaded with kayaks, they wear day-glow clothes and fluorescent sun screens. They're always trying to see you. It's bad P.R. You'd think it was one of these goat-oriented countries staging another demonstration."

"Really, sir. I don't know them."

"Well, see if you can't make them go away. Now, then. How's the project going?"

"Which one?"

"Teaching the Pakistanis to queue."

"Oh, that one. We're up against a tough one there, sir. You see, the British were here for a hundred years, and before they came these people used to line right up, but you know how the British are, sir. . . ."

---

[3] *Paddling the Frontier.* 1989, Travel Walji's.

The Swat was like a little seventeenth-century version of Switzerland: a conifer-covered alpine valley with a turquoise blue river coursing through it; rock-and-timber huts; goats and cows and drably dressed peasants wandering amiably about and through the excrement from all three species. There the parallel ends. It was a mountain resort for Pakistanis, but the valley was littered with hotels and trash; however, the worst pollution was audio.

Since elections were coming up, minivans overburdened with loudspeakers and bandwagon mobs plied the roads. Although the voices were distorted and in Urdu it was easy to understand what was being said: "Vote for me! I am an idiot!" (Loud cheers.) "I will fill my cabinet with idiots!" (Loud cheers.) "I promise you I will never bow to the fanatical, religious terrorism of Ayatollah George Bush!" (Extremely loud cheers.) "My opponent wipes boogers *on prayer rugs!*" ("NOOOO!") "I don't have boogers" (Loud Cheers.) Not only does my opponent listen to Western music, *he listens to Barry Manilow!* ("NOOOO!" Followed by sounds of mass puking.) "My opponent eats pig." ("NO!") "Vote for me and I promise you as many wives as you want!" (Loud cheers.) "Vote for me and I will flatten your taxes!" ("HUH?") "And let me tell you! Unborn children have rights too!" ("WHAT THE HELL IS HE TALKING ABOUT?") . . . And no sooner had that van passed when another began broadcasting in its dust; same old story, different title.

Even the presidency was at stake, but I wasn't certain why anyone would want the job. The retirement plan was lacking: Ali Bhutto had been hanged (which probably wouldn't be a bad idea for the last forty-two U.S. presidents, either, come to think of it. A simple swearing-in ceremony, followed quickly by a hanging-out party) and General Zia had died in a plane crash (PIA—Presidency In Abolition). One of the cantaloupes the plane was carrying had accidentally blown him to smithereens. (Later I was in Peshawar for the election. Unlike the U.S., where guns play a big part in the election, in Peshawar gunplay *is* a big part of the election. Bullets flew past my hotel window early into the morning. And when at last I ventured out into the street and discovered that civil war hadn't erupted after all, an earthquake struck.)

We put in the Swat at Kalam and were quickly surrounded by a crowd that seemed to be looking for an excuse to be hostile. The odd stone plunked down around us. Yousef (Joe for short), our main driver, had already warned us about these people. Just a few years before, Sunni Swat, holding Shia Gilgit in apostatic contempt for ending their Ramadan a day early, attacked. When the smoke cleared from this sectarian violence, several hundred lay dead.[4] Yousef said the number would have been three less if he hadn't been there.

"How do you know you killed them?" I kidded.

"No, dead! I made sure," he said in such a way that the hair on the back of my neck stood up. It was the first time I'd seen him smile since we arrived in this valley. Then he told me a word so bad he had to whisper it. He said to use it on the next person I saw. But I had no desire to start another war. Besides, I knew how this Swat bunch had already dealt with Alex the Great, sending him on his conquering way with what proved to be his fatal wound.

In fact, I couldn't even bring myself to use the word on a small child who was systematically dropping boulders on us at the take out. His face was one of perfect contentment, that universal happy curiosity that every child has as he slowly tortures a small, helpless animal into oblivion. Throwing rocks is merely a part of growing up in this valley. If you can't stone a bird or any other wildlife, you're a fat nothing. Releasing boulders onto kayakers is mere practice for the big time, like attacking Gilgit. Kids grow up far too quickly here and I didn't wish to rob this one of his youth. Chances were, by the age of fourteen, he would possess three or four harping wives, knock out six dozen kids, become a policeman, and lead a responsible, bribe-filled life. All I could do was shake my head at the injustice of it all. Here, with the election vehicles going around blaring nonsense, the kids had perfect targets for their rocks and instead they had chosen us.

After the Swat, most of the group returned to their diverse occupations, leaving only those of us who were gainfully unemployed: Andy Watt, the "alltouristic doctor" from Scotland, Mike Savory, Marcus, Slime, and myself. It was the perfect line to start a joke: "There was this Pakistani, a Kiwi, a Scotsman, an Irishman, an Englishman, and an American. Which one . . . "

As we drove down the Indus, the river's difficulty lessened as the plunge into it heightened. But this was just an academic point; an overloaded jeep dropping an extra five hundred feet wasn't going to make a lot of difference to us. Although traffic increased, allegiance to one side of the road or the other did not. At times I doubted that a feeler gauge would have fit between us and passing

---

[4] A suspect figure since many of these were probably annihilated in traffic accidents just trying to get to the violence.

vehicles. Buses and trucks were meticulously decorated with everything from woodcarvings to reflective tape; even the windows were ornamented to overindulgent degrees. Often the last thing a person sees in a head-on collision—and life—is the visually impairing sticker on the windshield of the oncoming bus which says: "I LOVE YOU." I feel, however, as drivers become more responsible, such meaningless stickers will be removed. And in their place will be one that reads: "How's my driving? Call 1-800 . . . "

As we left the Indus it began to rain. Because of the kayaks we couldn't put the top up. Joe flicked on the wipers and rendered our vision into a big muddy blotch. Further contributing to this feeling of lacking security there were our tires, all bald as Kojak—without a frown. So with smeared vision, barren tires, and steering as loose as change, Yousef, with the hollow look of a mass murderer in his eye, began speeding up.

"For Allah's sake, Joe!" I said, "Slow it down!" And Yousef did—but only for a few moments. Then Marcus wanted to stop to take a picture of a bridge.

"Please, sir," said Yousef, "It is best we do not stop."

"Why not?"

"Bandits. They are very bad here."

Despite rumors of banditry and terrorism, hostage-taking was not a problem. On good days I'd take three or four. [Hassen Bin Sober photo]

The road to the Kunhar River, where the word "precipitous" was invented. [D.B. Cooper photo]

We drove on in a strained silence that mingled into the road noise. Then Slime leaned over and said, "For Allah's sake Joe! Can't you go any faster?"

The next day, in friendly territory, we drove up the Kaghan Valley and Kunhar River (don't ask me how the wrong river got in this valley.) We proceeded to its headwaters and rented a room in a cold hotel that felt like an unpatrolled corner of a parking garage, a refuge for a wino. The next day it snowed, so we sat around and mutually falsified our diaries, then drove back downstream to find another hotel where Andy made a startling cross-cultural discovery. Although we begged him not to, Andy spoke Scots Gaelic. One night, listening to prayer call, he discerned numerous similarities to the verse of Scotland the Brave: "We want a bacon sandwich! They want a bacon sandwich! etc . . . "

We awoke to sunshine and a dandy run. Whether the people were friendlier or not, at least their rocks were poorly aimed.

The next day we attempted a gorge. That is, we attempted a road—which was a 2 and a 5 drive down to the gorge, a dirt tract scribbled down a near-vertical ridge, a place where the word *precipitous* surely was invented—a route that made all the other roads we had driven seem like excursions through Kansas. It was so steep, I even felt uneasy walking on it (in front of the jeep, of course, to show it where to go). At the river the gorge was dark and cold, and looked as inviting as an office with a downsized corporate executive in it.

Andy said, "I'm worried about the driver having to drive up that goat path by himself. I think for humanitarian purposes I'll accompany him. Besides, someone has to do it."

I said, "Andy, you're a brave man to go back up that road, I mean, not chickening out to go up a vile, hideous, dangerous road like

A typical truck. Although they should be in museums they are instead always in accidents.

◄ Our reception at Balakot, which led us to speculate that women are definitely not allowed on bridges in Pakistan.
► Shepherd. Kagan Valley

that. I'm worried, however, if you'll be all right. I'll accompany you."

Andy and I jeeped down past the river's carnivorous part then joined it and Slime, Marcus, and Mike once more. We paddled to the village of Balakot and here, above the final boulder garden, I asked Slime something I'd been wondering about for the last three weeks. I said, "Slime, you're the leader. What are you doing back here?"

"It's called hindsight."

"But hindsight is *after* the fact."

"Sure, you watch where everyone disappears in this next drop and avoid that spot. Follow me and you won't get in trouble."

"Slime, I've been trying to follow you for weeks now but you always grab and hog the last possible microscopic eddy above each drop. Anyone behind you is committed to a thrashing."

"That's experience."

We said goodbye to Yousef, tipping him with a tilt-o-meter for his jeep, and headed back to Pindi. Already, Marcus had shot 137 rolls of film on bridges. And besides, the authorities were getting wise to his cover as a kayaker. Two days later, worried about being arrested at the airport, he made his drop to another agent posing as a taxi driver—that is, Marcus left all his film and camera in the taxi.

Seriously though—and the reason I write this—is that Marcus *did* leave his film and camera in a taxi in Pindi. I later looked for this taxi when Marcus sent me a note saying that the driver's name began with "A." So I walked to the taxi driver's union office (because no taxi driver had a clue where it was, which also gives you an idea how powerful this organization is) and there I discovered that every taxi driver's name in Pakistan begins with "A." It is Muslim tradition—just like if you're born a Rothschild, you're rich; a Kennedy, you're a politician; a Deschner, you're independently lazy; a Muslim whose name starts with "A," you're a taxi driver. In other words, the film was gone. So please, if any one reading this has been to Pakistan and has any pictures taken of or from bridges, please send them to:

> Marcus Bailie
> Plas y Brenin
> Capel Curig
> Gwynedd
> LL24 OET
> Wales

I'm sure he will appreciate the junk mail.

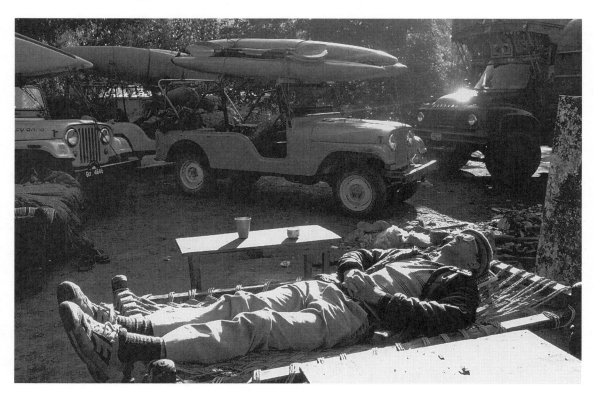

MARDI GRAS

And a Big Easy Swamp

◆ ◆ ◆

The last time George Bush ran for President he pledged, "Read my lips. No new Texas." Now flying over it, looking down, I couldn't even see who would want the old one; the one that gave us Lyndon Johnson, Willie Nelson, the Dallas Cowboys, the Savings and Loan Scandal, and George Bush himself. A conversation I had with several of my fellow passengers—a man, Tex; his wife, Huni (or Suga, I don't quite recall); and their seventh-grade son, Junior—only reinforced my feelings about the state. Tex and Huni ran memory seminars at the Alamo. Junior was busy draining the plane's Scotch and, despite his five-o'clock shadow at noon, I had to ask, "Aren't you a little young to be drinking?"

"I'm twenty-five years old!" he answered indignantly.

"And in the seventh grade?"

"Daddy and Mommy held me back so I could quarterback our junior high football team!"

Which made me start thinking positively about Texas, adding up its good points, such as: 1) I don't live anywhere near it; and 2) I was leaving it immediately.

At the airport, Tex, Huni, and Junior were whisked away in a block-long black limousine, while Carol met me in her multi-colored VW that was running on three cylinders. But hey! Any transportation to exit such a lone-star galaxy is worth honorable mention . . . Not that Louisiana looked any different. If it hadn't been for the welcoming sign and the change of roads, I wouldn't have been able to tell where Texas left off. In Texas there is more road than pothole; in Louisiana, it's the other way around. Even the Interstate is still in disrepair since it was last bombed during the War of 1812.

In time, but minus our suspension, we reached the Big Easy, New Orleans, which really was looking kind of old. Although billed as a historical city it is really a historical ruin. It was big all right but its easiness I

TRAVELS WITH A KAYAK

◀ Noted swamp Cajun
Jacques Le Strap.
[Carol Haslett photo]

never did figure out—like the problem of getting around. Most streets required a four-wheel drive. God help anyone trying to walk on the sidewalks; only rugged adventurers dare navigate them. Besides the city being in disrepair, it is also sinking. Real estate is not a good investment unless you are planning an underwater theme park. New Orleans is America's only city that employs bilge pumps.

Although I didn't research the following statistic, I think I can safely say there are two major occupations in New Orleans. Half the population supplies alcohol to the city while the other half serves it, and at this time of year—Mardi Gras—massive overtime was being put in. I could purchase anything on the street from daiquiris to beer. All a person had to do was approach any vendor, point, and say, "I'll have what that guy lying on the sidewalk is having."

Yet the city did have its own personality, especially in the French Quarter. Now, I pride myself in my education, that our public schools taught me to speak French with my nostrils clogged, and here at last I was able to utilize this contortion. Anyway, if you don't speak French[1] fluently like I do, you wouldn't know that "Mardi" means fat and "Gras" means Tuesday.

Some maintain that Mardi Gras runs year-round (and they look as though it does, too) but really it is the week leading to Mardi Gras when activity erupts. Various "krewes"—secret societies—have nothing better to do than spend all year building floats for their own individual parades. From these floats the krewes heave van-loads of necklaces to the crowd. Judging by the ensuing fights one can only deduce that New Orleans runs on a bead economy. Some krewes used to throw coconuts—that is, until the crowd started throwing them back. Now throwing coconuts is against the law and it is one of the most important amendments to the U.S. constitution: "Thou shalt not chuck coconuts at Mardi Gras."

Anyway, as each parade makes its way downtown, the crowd surges forward. The people standing in front try to grab as many beads as possible; the people in back shove those in front under the floats. In other words, just imagine a six-mile-long fraternity party, where you can meet many different, frat-like beings and hold interesting intelligent conversations like:

Me: "Hi, I'll bet you're from Smegma Phi Epsilon."

It: "Yeahaaaaaaaaaaaaahhhhhhh."

Even though large portions of the crowd look like recent

---

[1] I took three years of it in high school, received solid Ds, and not once was I taught, "C'est la vie." In case you were wondering, I got the same grade in English composition.

check-ins from Mars, most come to Mardi Gras from different states—and all wind up in one of drunkenness.

Evaluating what everyone was wearing—or not wearing—I quickly discerned that Southern Baptists have little influence here. That's not to say the festivities don't have religious roots, for the whole purpose of Mardi Gras is to give up lint for forty days. Everyone—women especially—are incessantly lifting their blouses to be checked; no lint brings great cheers from the crowd. Since the competition is stiff, many wear outfits that readily assure themselves attention. Yet many people, men and women, fearing the embarrassment of having lint found on their bodies, wear masks. And while on the subject of religion, I never—until New Orleans—had seen a nun in a see-through habit before.

Traditionally, during lint, it rains heavily for forty days and nights which, in the past, has caused certain doubting people, like Noah, to enter the shipwright business. Speaking of arks, this kind of inclement weather has had various effects on history, like the saga of Joan of Arc (naturally a person who could have used a good deluge once in her life). Involved in an exceptionally rowdy Mardi Gras known as "the Siege of Orleans," she sought refuge on the Lusitania, where she passed out, only to be awakened by a torpedo—the incident which, of course, brought the U.S. into the Rumpus of 1812. Sometimes history amazes me.

With Mardi Gras finished (by Tuesday, the city had immobilized itself in trash), we returned to our car—worried in such a crime-plagued city that it might not be there. But it was a senseless worry and, upon seeing it, we laughed at our foolishness. How could it go anywhere when someone had taken the wheels and the engine?

Later, after purchasing a few car parts, we picked up a canoe and traveled back west, heading for the Afchafalaya Swamp. (How do you say Afchafalaya? The best attempt is to say "alfalfa" and sneeze at the same time.) Having never been in a swamp before, I was curious and looked up its definition: "A place with lots of water, only more of it."

The first thing I noticed about the swamp was its overpowering aroma. "Fresh air!" I exclaimed.

"Did you just take off your shoes?" Carol asked.

This then, is Cajun country, the place where the Acadians found their final refuge after the British evicted them from Canada because they were always putting too much Tabasco in the jambalaya.

When the Cajuns came, they traveled down the Mississippi—well, maybe they traveled up the Mississippi. I don't really care. Then they headed off west in their pirogues across the Atchafalaya, which was an extraordinary undertaking when you consider that they could have used the freeway just a few miles to the north.

We were about to set off for a week. I don't know much about canoes, but I do know some fundamentals which are vitally important if you are planning a week-long trip. Basically, I've never liked canoeing because this species of boat never wants to go where I steer it. Add to this another person with her own ideas, and you've got a revolution on your hands. The important thing about canoes is to sit in the back, the end which learned people refer to as "the stern." There are several ways to do this. One, hop in and plead ignorance; say you thought it was the front (never say "bow," since this would give you away). Two, say, "Here! You take that end!" (meaning the stern). This should only be applied to people who are more civil and polite than you are, because they will react by insisting that you take the stern. Upon securing your place in the back, you get to steer the boat into rocks, trees, and other assorted debris. From this angle you can also watch your civil and polite partner grow flustered, angry, and, best of all, panicked. But more importantly, in the stern you don't have to work. I'm not suggesting you do no work; you must dip your paddle occasionally, often in unison with your partner. Entry is not important, and pulling is not a good idea; just make sure your paddle makes a loud noise as it exits the water. You might even say something like, "I do believe this is the slowest boat I've ever been in." The nice thing about the stern is that at the day's end, you appear hardly tired, a role model of modern fitness, while your partner feels like a mummy from an Egyptian Dynasty . . . Unfortunately, Carol was on to me, and she forced me to take the bow.

And so we set off into the swamp. Originally, we planned to take compass bearings, but immediately we saw that someone had marked the way with survey tape. An hour later we noticed that someone hadn't marked the way after all; they were actually marking their crawdad traps, and there were crawdad traps four-hundred-and-eighty degrees of the compass.

We spent the next week trying to figure out just where we were. At one point we even tried to log our headings: five minutes at 185 degrees, three minutes at 45 degrees, and so forth, which merely completed our confusion. Not that knowing a specific position in a swamp really matters, for it all looks the same.

Besides, we were not alone. The place was infested with Cajuns who had all sorts of opinions as to where we were. They are an easy-going sort, as anyone can see from their unique French dialect, a language spliced with occasional English, making it simple to speak. For example, note in the following dialogue how I have combined the French "bon jour," with the New Zealand English, "g'day."

"Bidet, mate!"

Now notice the Cajun's reaction.

"Regardez le shotgun."

Camping was sometimes a problem. Occasionally we'd find some high ground, at least three feet above sea level, a wonderful spot for a tent—but alas! Suddenly we were suffering from nose bleeds and had to retreat back to lower elevations and sponge-like earth.

Yet all our effort to get here (wherever that might have been) was well worth it, for I'd never seen a cypress swamp: the moss hanging from the trees, the silhouettes of cormorants. . . . In fact it was almost a prehistoric scene, and I could just picture a Tyrannosaur chasing a Bronchitis; a Stegosaurus engaged in mortal combat with a Thesaurus; a Pteranodon flying off with a Pictograph clutched in its talons. We saw armadillos, nutrias, alligators, herons, and snakes. Many people ask how you can identify the poisonous snakes. It's easy. They're the ones with at least three syllables in their names: water moccasin; cotton mouth; and diamondback rattler.

Eventually we arrived at St. Martinsville, the original colony of the Cajuns. It was here that Henry Wadsworth Longfellow came and sat under the famous Evangeline Oak. He thought of the Cajun's arduous struggle, their hardships, the harshness of the land, the love between a man and a woman with FATE wedged between them. A tear coursed down his cheek. Inspired, Longfellow picked up his pen, looked out across the swamp that the Cajuns had so laboriously traversed, then wrote:

> So be kind to your web-footed friends,
>
> For a duck may be somebody's mother,
>
> That lives in a place called a swamp,
>
> Where the weather is cold and damp!

Down and Out in

ALASKA

⬧ ⬧ ⬧

There are two theories to bush flying. One, go with a pilot who has never crashed, reasoning that they never—knock on wood, rub rabbit's foot, keep fingers crossed—will. Or two, go with an "experienced" pilot, one who has crashed and lived, because at least they know *how* to crash and survive.

Ted fit in the latter category. He fished out of the same camp I did, in Earth-left-field, Dillingham, Alaska. The first time I saw Ted's Piper Cub wrecked (though not the first time it had been in such a condition) was shortly after he buzzed the camp. The plane climbed, then started doing things I know Orville and Wilbur would not have endorsed. It spun and looped, emulating a county fair ride that spins you dizzy while hanging you upside down, until all the loose change is emptied from your pockets, before returning you to earth where you can throw up. When the plane finished this unwholesome behavior it returned to camp—and crashed.

As it turned out, Ted wasn't flying. At the controls was an old crop duster who hadn't flown in decades, whom Ted had inveigled into the pilot's seat. The duster remembered the aerobatics but forgot that he now wore bifocals and, misjudging the beginning of the camp runway, hit short, knocked the landing gear off, bounced airborne, leapfrogged the camp's fuel tanks that were kept in the runway's dogleg (not your normal runway), then returned to earth. Besides the crumpled landing gear, the impact bent the prop and scuffed up the underbelly. Otherwise the plane was intact. Unfortunately, this was not the last time I was to see the plane wrecked.

In subsequent years a few more mishaps occurred, like Ted failing a take-off here, flipping the plane beachcombing there, nothing much, just a few entries in a log book that was now looking like a catalog of disasters. Besides beachcombing, Ted actually did use the plane as a legitimate tax write-off, for example, to drop eggs on rival fishing boats.

On occasion, I had accompanied Ted on excursions and had actually survived, but the odds against me were growing. Ted would ask me to go with him on some new mission and I'd have to think up novel excuses to parry these invites, like, "Sorry, Ted, I've got to go see about this broken arm."

"But you don't have a broken arm."

"No, I'm about to go break it."

Ted was also a card-carrying gold junkie and he used his plane for prospecting. Often, while showing me his new riches, Ted would unscrew the cap on a vial no larger than a well-used pencil, then carefully spill the contents onto a piece of paper for me to admire. A single sneeze would have wiped out his earnings, along with our friendship. He'd always say, "There's more where this comes from."

Which was a relief, because what he always had wasn't much. What he was really hinting at, however, was for me to embark on some new airborne adventure with him, a hint I just plain ignored. Regrettably, he knew I possessed a weakness, too: I was a sucker for whitewater. Exploiting my addiction he nonchalantly inquired one day, "You want to go flying?"

I replied, "Ted, since it seems to be in the best interest of my continued existence, I've decided never to go flying with you again."

"Never?"

"Ever!"

"How about if I show you a creek that's never been run?"

"OK."

To get there, we flew over lakes and over alder- and spruce-brushed hills, then over hills that turned mountainous, jagged, and near-vertical. We were climbing and following a small creek when Ted, through the headset, voiced doubts about the weather and about a hide-and-go-seek hole in the cloud we needed to have open so we could clear the pass we were headed for. The rock shepherding our passage closed in. Ted said, "This is our last chance to turn around." But he kept going. Soon I was seeing details in the rock off both wing tips—details that I really didn't want to see. Buzzing just off the ground, we cleared the pass with our tail slicing the mists.

The land opened up, and Ted said, "Look on the map and see where we are now."

"Don't *you* know?"

"I haven't a clue."

"You mean we're lost?"

"No. We're not lost. I've been lost before and it looked nothing like this."

We followed a ribbon of a stream down until it petered out into a beaver-infested swamp.

"See where we are now."

"Don't you know yet?"

"Well we crossed some mountains back there."

This sort of conversation was normal with Ted. But every once in a while he dropped a bomb, like, "Just wait until you see where we're going, then you'll know why I didn't file a flight plan."

"You didn't file a flight plan?"

"You kidding? I didn't want anyone to know where we're going."

"Because of this unrun creek?"

"Well, no, not the creek. I didn't want anyone to know about this hot gold-panning spot we're heading to."

"You mean we're not headed for this creek?"

"Well, yes, but you don't just want to look at that."

"I don't?"

In time we arrived over, and correctly identified, Ted's unrun piece of water, Trail Creek. Its valley was broad, one large wrestling mat of tundra with a hundred-and-fifty-foot crack down its middle through which the creek ran. Heavily escorted by alder, the creek had the velocity of an excited slough.

"What do you think? Ted asked.

"I think I'm going to throw up all over your back if you keep cranking turns like this."

After checking out Trail Creek we hopped over some hills, landing on a strip called Canyon Creek, and arriving at a recently abandoned mine. We walked to an upthrust vein jutting through a small drainage. This was Ted's hot mother lode. Somehow I thought gold panning should be different. There was too much labor-intensive sloshing for the end product, which Ted referred to as "color," flecks of gold the size of fly poop that he painstakingly extracted with his forefinger. My idea was that if I couldn't extract the nuggets using my thumb and forefinger they weren't worth keeping. After half an hour of numbing my hands to such a state that I would never regain full control of my fingers, we extracted

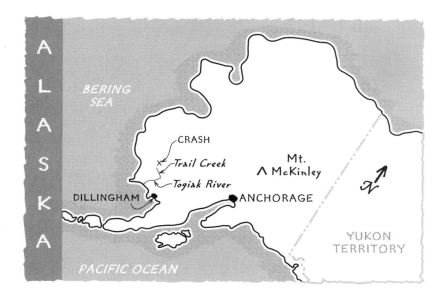

enough color to melt into a small nugget—not exactly enough to overburden and sink a Spanish galleon.

When at last our entire bodies were immobilized to the exact responsiveness of an ice cube (and richer by at least thirty-seven cents), we returned to the plane. Ted dumped a quart of oil in the engine and we took off. We flew south across a wind-blown ridge and Ted commented that it wouldn't be a bad place to land. It was too bad Ted didn't switch fuel tanks there, because, shortly after, over a place that *wasn't* good to land on, he did switch the fuel, and the engine quit.[1]

Dead.

In the void of the reassuring engine noise came the insidious sound of wind brushing the cabin as we began our disturbingly quick return to earth. But if I thought this sound was the lone thing that would unravel my composure I was wrong because suddenly I heard heavy breathing in the headset. Either Ted was practicing obscene phone calls or we were in for a heap of trouble. Then Ted, master of the understatement, announced, "This isn't good."

Time entered a new dimension. It ticked with rubber-second slowness, yet passed all at once. As we watched the unwelcoming terrain swell increasingly large we spotted a wind-eroded gravel ridge possibly big enough to accommodate a landing, a crash, or a combination of the two.

---

[1] As Ted explained later, "There was probably too much gas in the water."

But Ted, with two hundred feet to go, suddenly veered from the ridge and opted for a sloping piece of tundra. As soon as we turned, we fell, accelerating like a roller coaster—but there was no track awaiting us at the bottom. Out of sheer boredom on jets, I've read the safety card a thousand times: Get in a tuck position so that on impact you can drive your head through the kidneys of the person seated in front of you. It is a fine position if you are a yoga expert. But as I tried pressing my knees into my eyes I realized that the twits who write such cards have never been augured in a plane before. The problem is, you can't see. As I rose to watch, we hit.

I know my life passed before my eyes but I couldn't see it: Ted, flopping around like a Raggedy Andy doll, was blocking my vision. Instead, in what could have been my last moment on earth—as we were colliding back with it—I saw something akin to an atomic period Salvador Dali painting; everything was in suspension, only I was viewing it from inside a beer can being crushed. Plexiglass, a tire, and my hand all floated where plexiglass, a tire, and my hand shouldn't be; and these items were backdropped against a wing where a wing shouldn't be either. It was not a pretty picture, but one I came close to buying anyway.

Finally, the plane jarred to a stop, and quiet swelled around us. There seemed to be about a hundred-and-twenty-five decibels of it. Then Ted, wanting to make our exit as dramatic as possible, began smashing out the windshield with his fist—that is, until I opened the door.

We staggered from the wreck—25,000 uninsured bucks and now a useless crumpled heap. Ted shrugged and lamented, "Damn it, damn it, damn it! I just wasted a quart of oil!"

We sat there stunned, staring at the wreck, my knees clattering like castanets. At last I said, "Good thing for emergency locator transmitters."

"Oh yes!" Ted exclaimed, "I'd better turn it on!"

I said, "Let me get this straight. We have just crashed after not filing a flight plan and, on top of that, the E.L.T. wasn't armed?"

"Exactly. I never arm it. Every time I land too hard I set the darn thing off."

"Why weren't you born in the last century? You would have gotten on much better."

Ted turned the E.L.T. on, and our signal immediately snagged the attention of a passing satellite, which, in turn, immediately beamed the information to Control Central in France. France immediately exclaimed, "Voila! We have ze emarganzee sig-nal! Ted, ee must ave jaust land-ded hees plane ageen!" France immediately phoned Anchorage to let them know, and Anchorage immediately phoned Dillingham, which by this time had gone to bed. Dillingham, answering at last, said, "Do you know what time it is here?"

Late the following morning, above the cloud, we heard the distant drone of a plane circling. Ted grabbed the radio and, speaking in plane talk, said something like, "Distant drone of plane circling up there, this is voice of Piper Cub which has disassembled itself on the ground. Over."

"Yes, Piper Cub in pieces. Are you OK? Over."

"No. Situation critical. We need insect repellant immediately. Do you read?"

"Yes, copy that. Do you require anything else? Over."

"Yes. We're going to need some butter to fry these fish in."

Later in the day, having been given our coordinates, two friends, (in another Cub with no room for us), flew out to start our rescue. We flagged off a runway for them—the one we could have used. They brought us a loaf of bread, bug juice, a cube of butter, a can of Norwegian fish balls, and a 30-30 rifle. The pilot said he'd fetch us the next day.

However, on the morrow, the weather packed in, and for six days we saw no one. In the mornings we hiked down to the nearby creek and began fishing, with the intention of showing no mercy to the fish. However, the fish had already decided to show no mercy to us. Catching only one fish a day, and having wolfed down the bread, we resorted to blueberries. Reduced now to the status of hunter/gatherers, we immediately came across the fresh tracks of one of the local hunter/gatherers—tracks that one of our feet fit easily inside. We realized how inadequate our rifle was, should our competition decide to grow sensitive over the issue.

But later, starved, we came to realize that the rifle wasn't meant for bears at all but for use on ourselves, a realization that struck us when at last we opened the can of fish balls. We both swore we'd shoot ourselves before we were reduced to eating them.

Through the days of waiting, I began to comprehend that this fight for survival was something Ted had waited and practiced for his whole life. He was good at it, and if we'd stayed another week he would have constructed a five-bedroom log cabin, complete with a smokehouse and sauna. Ted caught all the fish. I lost the lures. Ted—even in the pouring rain—would carefully construct his fires with shavings and twigs, trying miserably to light them with a flint. While he was busy at this task, I'd be draining gas out of the wing into an open container. Returning to Ted's fire, I'd say, "Watch this!" and dump my fuel onto his twigs, then jump-start the whole shebang with a tossed match. Ted regarded such behavior as sacrilegious and I imagine that if we had been marooned one more day, Ted would have tried out the rifle on me. But I was spared, for on the sixth day, even though planes were still unable to reach us, a helicopter from a luxury fishing lodge at last fetched us. Even industrial detergent couldn't have resurrected the leather

Ted's Cub suffering from one of the downfalls of aerial scouting, while Ted contemplates the quart of oil he just wasted.

seats after they were smeared by our grime-covered clothes.

Soon, we were back in the narrow confines of town, and the even narrower confines of the town's cafe—with several dinners stacked in front of us. There, a local asked what we were doing up Trail Creek. It was tough getting an answer out through all the food we were stuffing into our faces. But when he understood our reply, the local, firing a Parthian shot, informed us that we'd be hard pressed to make a first run down Trail Creek.

"Why's 'at?" I asked, filtering the words through a mouthful of whipped potatoes.

"Why, don't you know? Jacky Smeaton wrecked his plane up there years ago and made a boat out of a tarp and willows and floated out."

INDONESIA

Endo-Nesia and Bali-Low

The French railways would not then take a canoe as baggage, while the other seven or eight countries we had brought the boat through were all amenable to pressure on this point, but the French too are wiser now, since other paddlers have journeyed there.

—John MacGregor, A *Thousand Miles in the Rob Roy Canoe*, 1881

◆ ◆ ◆

One winter, spinning wheels, I found myself passing through a squalid little third-world country. Fortunately, I had a friend who lived there—a boater, no less—and I called ahead to say I'd be dropping in.

"How's Boise these days?" I asked.

"The black market exchange rate is off, but with the Republicans coming to power, it should skyrocket soon. Make sure your gun is loaded. The sagebrush is revolting here."

"I know," I said, "I see they already changed the welcome sign from 'Idaho is too great to litter' to, 'Idaho is too iliterate to be great.'"

He went on to say he was having a party that night and I should stop in.

And what a party it was! The men were all drinking Dos Equis and getting cross-eyed. The females had removed their veils, revealing their sheepish looks. I'd never seen such good-looking sheep in my life. Unfortunately, they were more interested in the condiment table, which they all had herded around sticking celery sticks in the sheep dip. My host handed me a beer, and I soon felt I was blending right in. We sang a round of *fle-eece navidad* (although I don't think the sheep got the joke) and when it was over someone asked me what I was doing for the rest of the winter.

◄ Carol on the Baliyan—or the Ayung. At least I know I took this shot somewhere on Bali.

"Going to Costa Rica to boat," I replied.

He slapped his gut as if he'd been shot—and I wasn't so sure he hadn't been—when he fell to the floor laughing. Someone else asked him what was so funny.

"He's going to Costa Rica to boat!" came the reply between gales of laughter.

Several more people burst out laughing, crumpling to the floor helplessly, and soon everyone but the sheep (who were looking pretty nervous) were on the floor laughing, repeating, "He's going to Costa Rica to boat!"

Only later, *much* later, after the last sheep had been fleeced, did I learn that I had unintentionally told one of the funniest jokes

ever: In January and February, Costa Rica has little water.

Now most boaters would say, "Well, for starters, I won't stop in Boise again," and, "I'll just travel somewhere that *does* have water." So I re-aimed my sights on Indonesia, a place I knew even less about than Costa Rica. I returned home to study my atlas. Indonesia's unmistakable shape looked like an unchecked sneeze on a blank page.

I bought my ticket the next day. Although I requested Bali, the destination was to a place that sounded like a malaria prophylactic.

It had been several years since I had flown with a kayak, and I quickly discovered that airports had changed. With frequent-flyer programs, airports were busier. Unfortunately, since several ethnic

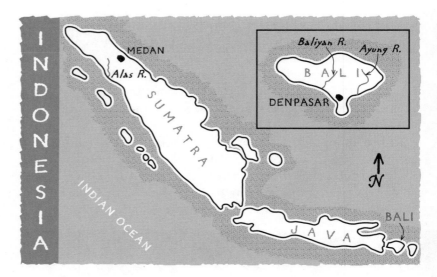

groups were being excluded from getting frequent-flyer cards, they were threatening to blow up the planes. This meant that any odd piece of luggage—like a kayak—was quickly regarded as a large bomb. Also, I had to deal with a life-form named Red.

In the past, every Red I had ever met was strictly cow-oriented. They never exceeded a room temperature IQ, and the thought of one working in an airport would permanently ground any aerophobic—but when Reagan deregulated the country back into the dark ages, all that changed. Now don't get me wrong about Reds. At one time, many have had triple digit IQs, along with names like Joe, Bob, Mike, John, or Dave, but inevitably, a horse had thrown them head first onto an unsympathetic rock, and forever after they were known as Red—by their friends: Corky, Butch, and Buster.

Red said, "We don't take kayaks."

"Ha!" I laughed, "Who said anything about kayaks? This is a Topolino![1] See it says so right here T-o-p-o-l-i-n-o."

Unfortunately, this was no time to give Red a spelling lesson. His foam-ringed lips tried repeating the name but it only came out in post-Pithecanthropus—but definitely pre-Neanderthal—grunts.

"Look," I said, "Do you take skis?"

"Yes."

"Surfboards?"

"Yes."

"Well this is a surf ski."

---

[1] A stubby but buoyant kayak (pictured on p. 190) popular in Europe for steep creeks—and because they fit on stubby cars.

This knitted Red's brow, but then he announced, "You can't fool me! That's a kayak!"

"I already told you it's not. It's a Topolino. Means Mickey Mouse in Italian. Sort of like your airline when they hired you."

But, alas, flattery will get you nowhere, except (if you keep it up) the security guards. After half an hour of this kind of talk, I at last asked to talk to a supervisor.

"I am the supervisor," Red informed me. "We don't take kayaks."

"Ha!" I laughed, "Who said anything about kayaks? This is a Topolino! See, it says so . . . "

But never mind. Suffice it to say that at last my kayak was taken. Suffice it also to say that the next person who tries to slip a Topolino past Red, won't.

Red, who reluctantly let me on the plane, punished me with the responsibility of an emergency exit. Fortunately, my flight was emergency free. Unfortunately, it was marred by a theft. The pilot informed everyone that we were crossing the dateline—the oldest gag in the book and I fell for it. I looked out the window at the dotted line running through the ocean, and when I looked back an entire day had been stolen from me.

In time—but missing a day—I arrived at Denpasar, the Malaria Prophylactic International Airport. Immediately upon disembarking I was exposed to Customs—strange Indonesian ones. At a large table men in uniforms wearing toy Uzis dumped out women's suitcases, rummaging through them while holding contests to see who could find the skimpiest underwear and the most embarrassing sex toy. When these festivities ended, we were released to a welcoming committee of taxi drivers—or roughly 90% of the population of Bali. Fortunately, one of the attributes of traveling with a kayak is that these knuckleheads quickly leave you alone. Unfortunately, one of the negative aspects of traveling with a kayak is that when you do demand a cab, you're going to be pegged for roughly seventy-nine times the normal fare.

It was 3:00 a.m. by the time I arrived at a hotel. I couldn't sleep; both familiar and foreign sounds dropped into the darkness. There was distant surf, crickets, the redundant coo-cooing of a pigeon, a yapping dog (one I wanted wokked) the two-tone squeeze/squeak of geckos, the insidious hum of a blood-laden mosquito trapped inside my mosquito net, and a rooster who all night crowed reveille for every dawn across the Pacific, except for his own, which he was too worn out to announce. Instead it was heralded by a lonely Muslim prayer call. Light soaked up dark and I gazed at the geckos stalking prey on the ceiling. Spiderman is a misnomer, I thought, then succumbed to sleep.

That afternoon, finally awake, I procured an aspiring new driver (Wayan, meaning "the annihilator" in Basa Indonesian; "John" for short) who, desperately wanting work, charged me a mere thirty-six times the going rate. Unfortunately—as the numerous dogs, pedestrians, bicyclists, and motorcyclists that we subsequently hit could attest—John was still learning. This fact was compounded by his car, a Holden, so ancient that was licensed as a historical monument.

It was so cancered with rust it could be push-started from inside. All you had to do was extend your feet through the hole where the floor used to be and, à la Fred Flintstone, run. It was a multiple feature for when the car did get going, the extended foot method was also one of the frequently engaged braking options. The hole also acted as a flow-through air conditioner. The air simply flowed through where the floor used to be, exiting where the windows used to be. As for the steering wheel, it was still there but I'm not sure what function it served, since the direction it was turned often had nothing to do with the direction the car was heading. But that was not always bad considering the bizarre ways John tried turning it.

Even now I cringe when I think back on John's Holden and his handling of it, but the alternative way of getting around was even worse. Yes, I'm talking about the dreaded Bemos which means matatu in Swahili and canned herrings in Norway. Bemos are surplused Japanese school buses, built for children under the age of five and carrying six times the limit of full-size adults. Bemos rarely travel to any planned destination. They merely pick up loads of passengers, charge them exorbitant and arbitrary fares, then drive them as quickly as possible into the end zone of all their sensibilities. This is accomplished by the conductor a) tightly sealing all windows, which increases the inside temperature to spontaneously combust the cigarettes everyone is holding; b) releasing large quantities of flatulence; and c) the conductor playing the song, *Feelings*, on the tape deck, which causes the passengers to abandon the vehicle by all possible means and regurgitate in unison into rice paddies.

Of course, people can listen to *Feelings* so many times before they run amuck. The word "amuck" is of Malay invention and is used to describe those who have regurgitated into rice paddies one too many times. Amuck symptoms are easy to spot: a thousand-yard stare, similar to and often confused with the one employed by those who have just had dealings with an insurance agent; strange, incomprehensible sounds often employed by those who have just imbibed large quantities of alcohol; and the waving of a large knife through the space occupied by unfortunate bystanders. As you can discern, Indonesia is an extremely primitive and barbaric nation, completely unlike the U.S., where civilized, disgruntled employees can—with semi-automatics—simply spray bullets at random into civilized co-workers.

Which makes me think of the impassioned testimony before Congress I once heard by an old man who had developed the shakes. On bended, arthritic but shaking knees, he pleaded for his constitutional right to keep his semi-automatic rifle. Otherwise, how the hell was he going to hit large animals while out hunting? The speech quickly brought tears to one's eyes—and a strong desire to live in a concrete bunker and wear bullet-proof pajamas.

But I digress: I was writing about uncivilized Indonesia.

The first known reported case of anyone running amuck in Indonesia was Alfred Russel Wallace. He ran amuck for years, annihilating everything from the docile butterflies of Bali to the wild men of Borneo. The outcome of this random slaughter was the theory of evolution, which proved beyond a doubt that Charles Darwin evolved from a Beagle. Coincidentally, Wallace is also famous for the Wallace line. He used it repeatedly to pick up Australian nurses in various Bali nightclubs.

After more time, John drove me to my first river, the Baliyan. Here I refer to my notes:

Well! Guess I didn't take any! Anyway, there's a river on Bali somewhere called the Baliyan. John knows where it is and you can ask him where the put-in is. You can't miss the take-out, though. It's a large, shark-infested body of water, and if you get past the breakers you've gone too far.

Next, John's Holden—with little help from John—took me to the Ayung, which was so much like the Baliyan I won't describe it here (see above notes). In fact, I'm not sure it *wasn't* the Baliyan, just higher up. The local rafter described the river as paradise, which is pretty much what you'd expect from a rafter. I personally witnessed several sewers entering, greatly subsidizing the flow, but fortunately, the smell was pleasantly masked by a dead water buffalo which helped form one of the rapids.

Besides, I didn't have time to notice river detail, for at that moment, on the banks of the Ayung above, a far more interesting development was taking place. There, perched in what a rafter would claim was an idyllic setting, was a man with two jealous wives—although I suppose the word jealous is highly superfluous. The man had a successful history. He'd worked hard and sown his plans carefully; eventually they blossomed into the ownership of a large, thriving hotel. Wanting to share his success, he married; his hotel business blossomed some more and wanting to share his further success, he married again. At first, he was the envy of the neighborhood, for everyone knew he didn't need reservations to stay in his hotel, and that his wives were very beautiful, and that they had yet to learn the pleasures of using Visa or MasterCard. Then one day he made a fatal mistake. He accidentally gave wife #1 a pen. It was nothing much, just an old Bic ballpoint that only spread ink when it was in a shirt pocket. But wife #1 told #2 about it, along with the Malay, "Nyah nyah nyah-nyah nyah-NyaH!" In an instant the man's happy life was diminished to a case study for Amnesty International.

In hopes of appeasing wife #2, he gave her a clicking ballpoint. And she was appeased, too, only she informed #1 of the fact in a manner that #1 did not take kindly to and six months later, when I came kayaking past, the war had escalated into something that not even the U.N. could further help escalate with negotiations. Some enterprising local stopped me and, for a nominal fee, offered to show me this doomed man. He escorted me into a secret passage of the hotel and then, fearful of being caught, directed me to a one-way mirror.

Expecting to see the living definition of doomed, I was surprised to see a smirky-faced guy who looked much like myself. "Ya poor bugger," I thought, "bet you had a rough time getting a date in high school." Then I wondered what he did with his dates when he did get them. I know what I did with mine. Late at night I took them to a very expensive jewelry store and told them that if they pressed their face up against the glass door they would see a necklace with enough carats to equal the Gross National Product of a small country like, say, Canada. My dates would sort of coo romantically, thinking I was dork enough to work as a lifelong indentured servant to make payments on such foolishness—at which point, seemingly from nowhere, the guard dog would hit the bulletproof glass with the velocity of a surface-to-air missile. I can never remember having the same date twice.

And as I looked through that mirror feeling sorry for this pathetic creature, someone tapped me on the shoulder and whispered in my ear: "You're looking at the wrong side of the mirror."

I never did see the man. When I was there he had just finished building a second restaurant, which #1 had insisted upon owning—followed, of course, by #2 wanting one also. The only problem with eating at either restaurant was that guests had to order and eat the same thing in the other wife's restaurant. For awhile it appeared the situation had reached equilibrium, but no, someone went and ordered an extra Diet Pepsi and once again there was massive escalation. Currently, (five years later) I have heard each wife is now demanding a nuclear power plant and that the Americans have offered to buy one for wife #1 since the Russians have promised #2 a deal she can't refuse.

Without regrets I left paradise. I wanted to go to Borneo to boat because then I could write an article called "Kayaks and Dayaks," but unfortunately, you can't go to Borneo any more because, like Burma and Ceylon and Peking, it doesn't exist. Instead I flew to Medan, Sumatra, which is, unfortunately, still there.

With its going rate of four-hundred clams, Medan is supposedly one of the cheapest cities in Asia to have a person bumped off in. Traffic, though, will do the same thing for free. Crossing the street I was instantly reduced to a Nintendo target. Back on the relative safe sidewalk, a skinny man sold various animal parts to fortify the bodies of those tired of having sand kicked in their faces. And if that didn't work, his fat neighboring vendor offered a spread of human teeth to replace those removed from fighting bullies.

I hired a taxi to do the Alas, which in Malay means *really, really, really* boring river—just one of the many words I'd learned from reading my Indonesia/English and vice/versa text. Just to give some idea of what my Indonesian must have sounded like, here are some of the choicer excerpts from my phrase book:

I want a guide who can speak English.
I am, but I know a little English.
It is never mind.
The important one is you understand what I speak.

Is your girlfriend beautiful?
No she is rather ugly.

Is your boyfriend handsome?
Yes, he is strong too.
This is a new thing.

At the dentist:
Patient: Indeed you are hurting me!
Doctor: I am sorry. Well, I want to do it slowly.

Since I had only phrases like these to depend on, the car and driver I ended up with came as no surprise. I never did learn the driver's name. I was too terrified to engage him in such deep conversation. Besides, communication was impossible for he owned a single tape and he played it repeatedly at full volume. This Genghis Khan facsimile's sole aim in life was to destroy all forms of eastern civilization as he knew them. For this vehicular genocide, Genghis applied only one technique: Once the vehicle is moving, the accelerator must never, under any circumstance, leave the floor, not even through ditches or cornfields or pig sties (hey, what are *they* doing in a Muslim country?) where we frequently ended up, through no fault of our own, but that of the complete idiots who insisted on driving on their side of the road. The roads contained potholes as big as mine shafts, and I'm not so sure some of them *weren't* mine shafts. I am certain, though, that more than one kid has fallen into them, never to be seen again. Not that it would be any great loss, for the area could afford to lose a few kids—like about six million. Currently, there seemed to be a plague of them going on. All I saw was kids. We passed through numerous rubber plantations, and I could certainly see what the rubber *wasn't* being used for. We passed various churches and mosques, the corrugated tin roofs denoting the two religions, their spires inviting the heavens to fry entire congregations with nondenominational lightning strikes.

Eventually, we came to the Alas, along with the Lesser Gunnig National Park and Insect Reserve. It used to be called More Gunnig N.P. before most of the park's trees were cut down. The park was created solely for the preservation of international research workers, and locals come from miles around to spot the various scientists from countries that no longer have enough scientific habitat to support them. Fortunately, these researchers round

Indonesian Tour de France entrant.

out the food chain nicely, supplying much-needed meat for the local insect economy. Just because all the trees are gone doesn't mean the area is devoid of wildlife. Kayaking through this section, I spotted many cockroaches, several real estate agents, homeless houseflies, industrial-sized mosquitoes, King Cole gnats, sleeping-bag bugs, earwigs, several Whigs without ears, and the unidentifiable phantom of the Lepidoptera. It quickly brought back everything I ever learned in biology: Fruit flies like a banana; time flies like an airplane.

From the park the river issued into an area that looked a lot like the park but wasn't the park, because this area had people living in it—unlike the park, which had temporary people living in temporary housing that had been set up with temporary gardens which were surrounded by trees which had been temporarily cut down. As a researcher advised me, the boundary was discernable by the density of kids replacing the density of insects, however, not having a scientific Wallace-like eye, I had trouble distinguishing the difference.

With my superb mastery of the language, I asked this worker, "Does this river have any piranhas in it?"

To which he replied: "No, the crocodiles ate them."

For the next day the river was extremely boring, with the exception of places where it was tedious and others where it was monotonous, which in turn were punctuated by dull, flat, and all-around-dead stretches. Kids, whom I had come to identify more readily, mainly because there were forever more of them to identify—were never more than a stone's throw away. Helmets are necessary on this river. That evening the river cranked a hard right, one so abrupt I nearly missed it, and the river entered the jungle. At least it entered where the jungle was *supposed* to be. When I arrived the locals—when they weren't busy making kids—were participating in the other national pastime: slashing and burning up the jungle. At least the smoke made for a very spectacular sunset.

The following day I descended into raw virgin jungle that had not yet had its behavior modified. Basically, the whole ecosystem looked exactly like toe jam under a microscope—and smelled like it also. All the documentaries I'd ever seen on jungles had it wrong, for the main character couldn't have swung more than two feet on a vine without encountering large, dense splotches of vegetation. With the exception of a red-leafed tree that looked like an autumn sumac on steroids, the color of this verdure was always the same thick broccoli evergreen. Up close, Mother Nature's cookie cutter had worked hard on the leaves, variegating them into every size and shape imaginable. As for animals, the largest I ever saw was a kingfisher, one that made the American brand seem a sorry representative of its species. This kingfisher had a tan breast and appeared to be wearing an iridescent blue tuxedo. In color and shape, its beak looked like a carrot. Wallace would have shot it. There was no abundance of roaring and terrifying large animal noises to perpetually remind Diaper Man of the fact he was not kingpin of the food chain. The riot of noise issued solely from insects—which would have regarded his mostly naked body as lush open range—and his cry would never have risen above them. The din came mainly from cicadas; however, some of the racket was produced by unidentified bugs, like the one that sounded similar to a chain saw, which was followed by another bug imitating a tree falling. I just don't see how Jane would have stood for it. *I* certainly couldn't and so I left the next day, my desire to paddle jungle rivers brought to a quick finish.

Carol, bored with the Alas, tries to flag down a ride. Hearing that we hadn't enjoyed the trip the locals stoned us at the take-out, thus eliminating any doubts we had left.

Our daily allotment of water (25,000 cfs, personally passed by the dam inspector), being released.
[Bureau of Reclamation photo]

GRAND CANYON

Nightmare On Helm Street

Good Temper.—Tedious journeys are apt to make companions irritable one to another; but under hard circumstances, a traveller does his duty best who doubles his kindliness of manner to those about him and take harsh words gently, and without retort . . .

— Francis Galton, *Art of Travel*, 1872

❖ ❖ ❖

I grew up some overseas. Being the new kid on the block, I was often asked, even before there was an exchange of names, if I had ever been to Disneyland. When I said no I was immediately discounted as not being an authentic American. Several years later I did get to Disneyland but by then it was too late.

Four more years passed and I went boating abroad. Being the new boater in the eddy I suddenly heard an old script repeating itself, only the name had been changed. Had I run the Grand Canyon? No, but I had been to Disneyland.

❖ ❖ ❖

Forget all the windbags who have written about the Colorado's "life-threatening rapids," the problem with the Grand Canyon is its name. It is the epitome of American hype. *The Super Bowl, the World Series, The Breakfast of Champions, The Sale of the Century—The Grand Canyon.* Really, what we are dealing with here is a Large Eroded Trench in the Earth's Crust. But Large Eroded Trench in the Earth's Crust National Park hardly cuts the cheese; that is, if you wish to lure the masses and make them believe they have really seen it all. That is fine for the average tourist who drives to the South Rim and spends an emotion-filled forty-five minutes: five minutes videoing grandma and the whining kids, and the remaining forty looking for the gift shop, rest rooms, and Fluffy, who just fell into the canyon. But for the thousands of boaters who wish to become intimate with this giant erosion problem and spend two to three weeks running the river, problems arise.

Take Carol's case, for example. Wanting to go privately she applied for her permit when she was not yet born; thoughtful parents put her on the waiting list. Forty-three years later she could at least guess the decade in which her trip might begin. This was no small accomplishment since at arbitrary intervals she had had to fill out bales of new forms from the Park's Redundancy Department of Redundancy to let them know that yes indeed, she was still interested in running the river. This correspondence amounted to an almost thousand-dollar investment in stamps—not counting the skin graft she had to get on her tongue after licking them.

"Sometimes," Carol once exclaimed as she was dealing with yet another batch of forms, "I think some of these people were given their bureaucratic procedural training in India."

When at last she received her starting date a new problem arose: Those of her friends who hadn't died in the meantime were busy procreating instead of recreating (and since they no longer kayaked she considered them as good as dead). After licking another 485 stamps she came up with a manifest of eleven people, mostly strangers, who all seemed liked sensible human beings (with the possible exception of Dave Manby, one of the few Carol and I both knew). And then . . . .

The Grand Canyon Office of Whimsical Regulations canceled her trip. After Carol had subsidized the U.S. Postal Service for 43 years, her last 29-cent installment, the one confirming her trip, got held up because George Bush had flown all the way from Disneyland to have his picture taken in front of the Grand Canyon.[1] Fearing that someone might mail George a get-well card with a bomb in it, the Park Service shut down their post office. The real bomb went off when Carol learned of her trip being scratched. Unfortunately, by then, George had left.

Then there was a further set of problems: the trip itself. Carol,

---

[1] Actually, a picture of him leaping into the canyon would have been far more spectacular.

after having her trip reinstated, finally arrived at Lee's Ferry, where she met her rag-tag group.

Since the Grand Canyon lives in a sacrosanct theme park class of its own, special rules have been designed to protect it. These rules are spelled out in a set of books slightly surpassing the O.E.D. in length, and before our party could get wet we had to be indoctrinated. This meant being oriented towards the orientation building and, once we were oriented towards the front of the room, orientation took place. I note here some of the prominent rules:

☞ All Dutch ovens must have adequate Coast-Guard-approved flotation. People don't realize how many Dutch ovens there are at the bottom of the Grand Canyon, and by the year 2000 if people don't stop losing them, the nature of the rapids will have changed dramatically.

☞ Although pets are not allowed, Seeing Eye dogs are, because, of course, how else could a blind person see the Grand Canyon?

☞ Seeing Eye pigs are also allowed. Pigs are good because with one along there is no need to bring a toilet—and on the last night the pig can be eaten.

☞ If no pig is brought then the contents of all rocket boxes shall be properly disposed of in McDonalds' dumpsters.

☞ Fires during off-season are for aesthetic purposes only.

☞ A few rules cover those who run the joint, some more apply to commercial rafters, and all of them apply to private parties.

☞ All articles written on the Grand Canyon must be written in chronological order and must be of an introspective, search-for-self nature. (Question: Where do I throw up?)

DAY 1. October 15. Lee's Ferry, named after the Mormon scapegoat John D. Lee. Not seeing much future in wiping out wagon trains, Lee moved here to gouge the settlers in a new way, but in 1877 he was executed for overcharging on his ferry.

Reconfirmed the rumor that a constant flow of 25,000 cfs is false. This rumor was started the day after the dam was built and has been in circulation ever since.

All day I have forced myself not to wonder about some of the members of this group. However, this evening my attitude has shifted. Pulling into camp, one of our three rafters sent his girlfriend rushing into the bushes to claim the best real estate for their tent. In the meantime, this same rafter sat deeply immersed in thought while engaging in mortal combat on his pocket Nintendo. Another rafter simply unloaded a lawn chair (the only one on the trip) and a Michener book, *Boise*, sat down, and began to read while the rest of us unloaded his raft. With such suspect behavior starting already, I hope this trip will unfold into a good one. Somehow, I am struck with a strange sense of déjà vu.

DAY 2. Two out of our three rafters continue to worry me. Both specimens are commercial guides, both seem to have grown up in the same weed patch—and they remind me of yet another of their kindred. That particular self-commissioned deity arrived at my house once with a twenty-dollar bill; he wore a pair of jeans and a T-shirt, and for the time he stayed—the exact period of a nuclear winter—he changed none of them.

At mile 12 we passed the 1889 inscription denoting where Frank M. Brown drowned while surveying the canyon for a railroad. Of course it was never built but one wonders, if it had been, how many private departures the Park Service would allow per day? Anyway, the point is that rivers and railroads don't mix; however, up in Smithers, B.C. (where the locals are known as "Smithereens") I did run once into a train engineer who kayaked.

I showed this engineer a map of the Babine, which I was about to run, spreading it out with north facing up—but no sooner had I done so when the engineer adjusted it askew.

I corrected his orientation, but immediately he reoriented my reorientation.

"I believe it goes like this," I finally said, turning it back once more.

But he turned it again and asked me, "Water flows down hill, doesn't it?"

"Well, yes," I replied after an astonished pause. "But there's a north to maps."

"Ah, what the hell! I never read them anyway. I drive trains. I just follow the tracks."

"What about rapids?" I asked.

He gaped at me as though my mind were derailing, then he said, "There's no rapids on the tracks!"

DAY 3. Actually, the people in Smithers don't talk like that at all, but rather they speak in questions. For example, a typical wedding ceremony climaxes with the bride and groom proclaiming, "I do?" And forever after they question their judgment.

Because everyone answers each other's questions with a question, very little gets done in Smithers—which is why the town remains small. The first conversation I ever had there went like this:

"Where are you going?" a local asked.

"The Babine."

"The Babine?"

"Yes, the Babine."

"Oh! that's nice?"

"Is it?"

"It is?"

"I don't know, I'm asking."

"It is?"

"I told you I don't know."

"I'm telling you?"

"You are?"

"I am?"

Damn it, I'm digressing, but it's just that all these intermittent snow showers we are having in the canyon remind me of my trip on the Babine. To temporarily escape this inclement weather we stopped at Red Wall Cavern. Major Powell thought this cave could seat 50,000 people, which just goes to show how much smaller people were in those days.

This evening two particular rafters received—behind their backs—new names. With us now is Gan Moondork, one of Nintendo's escaped mutations; his woman, the Rubber Dummy; and the Sloth, clearly a victim of one too many mescal worms. Upon landing this evening, Gan, is once again playing Nintendo while the Rubber Dummy ran to grab the best tent site. Meanwhile the Sloth forsook his book and instead crawled ashore to sleep—while we unloaded his raft.

Later, we built an aesthetic fire upon which we cooked aesthetic steaks along with the rest of an aesthetic meal. Afterwards, around aesthetic coals, Dave Manby—while passing non-aesthetic gas—spoke of his current sponsorships, which explains why he wears a papal vestment while eating with Mexicana Airlines silverware out of a dog dish.

DAY 4. Camped tonight at some remains of Bert Loper's[2] boat: a bowsprit, a mizzen top gallant, and a hard chine. As my eyes rose from this historical trash onto the canyon's cliffs I couldn't help but think: If only these walls could talk. The things they would say! Just imagine the first, astonished words of the Native Americans who stumbled onto the canyon: "Oh, my gosh! How the heck we ever gonna get across *this* ditch?" And later, the tension of Powell's men as they struggled desperately for survival in the canyon's depths: "Flush beats a straight, don't it?" But probably the choicest tales would come even later, when the tourists began floating the river: "Oh, my goodness!" Suzy gasped through wet, moist lips. Suzy had just abandoned her idiot husband in camp and, even more recently, her clothes on a nearby bush and, now, standing naked in a pristine grotto with John, she stared at his enormous swelling . . .[3]

Well, I guess it's best the walls don't talk after all!

DAY 5. Camped by the fo'c's'le of B'rt L'per's bo't. We didn't see any other people today but we did run into some scientists. They said they were studying erosion. I asked if they weren't several billion years too late. Scientists did not laugh. Seems if they really want to study erosion, they should go watch all the bagfuls of "pretty" rocks being hauled away at the take out. If you wish to enjoy the Grand Canyon in color, do so quick; in ten more years it will all be in black and white.

DAY 6. Since this is the off season, only the Park Service is running motorized rigs, and the number of commercial launches is down to 65 a day. The positive feature of the off season is that the weather is cooler, like today. It is 35 degrees Fahrenheit and the wind is blowing up the canyon at 87 m.p.h., which adds to a wind chill factor of—let me refer to my chart—"Should not be skiing," which is good, because we aren't. The cooler climate also brings up a negative aspect: You don't see as much wildlife, like rattlesnakes, scorpions, and tarantulas. I'm not fond of interfacing with wildlife anyway, which brings up an old incident at Victoria Falls.

There, on the Zambian side, in back of a hotel, I discovered a kayak and I asked the caretaker if I could take it for a spin. I wanted to paddle out to Livingstone Island and peer over the falls from the middle. The caretaker was hesitant, and

---

[2] Bert, age 79, died of boredom in 24^1/$_2$ mile rapid in 1949 while reading James Michener.

[3] Ego. John was a commercial rafter.

although he couldn't speak English, he did manage to say, "No problem." At least that's what I *thought* he said.

Since the river was at near-flood stage, drifting down to the island would be simple; however, fighting the current back upstream could prove to be a vain struggle. So instead, not to be defeated, I decided that any island would do, and I ferried toward Zimbabwe to an island lacking a front-row view of the falls. As I paddled away, the caretaker began waving at me enthusiastically and I commented to myself what a friendly fellow he was. Landing on the island I immediately noticed hundreds of large round footprints and I muttered, "Funny, I wonder what all these elephants were doing out here?"

When I returned back to the Zambian shore, the caretaker greeted me with such relief his face had the symptoms of Prozac overdose. Someone who spoke English stood next to him and asked me, "Do you know how many hippos are out there?" Instantly I felt as if I'd received a Jello transfusion.

Turned out the caretaker had not only *not* lent me the kayak but had warned of the danger as well. He had spoken two complete sentences. "No," and, "Problem."

DAY 7. We have at last cracked the tide mystery. A *TV Guide* dropped out of Gan Moondork's bag and, by cross-referencing the flows with the programs, we can not only accurately predict the tides, but we can also rate the TV shows better than Nielsen.

DAY 8. Camped (Bert Loper's gangway) at the historical site where the first jet stream was spotted in 1956. Upon opening dry bags we found that all three thousand of the trip's bagels were soaked.

At certain moments the canyon seemed extremely note-worthy. It reminded me of my neighbor, a rancher. Because I kayak, he asked me to accompany him on a jet-boat ride down Hell's Canyon, a place he'd never been, even though it was less than sixty miles from his ranch. Now, my neighbor knows everything there is to know about ranching. He knows, for example, that the quickest way to a cow's heart is through all four of its stomachs; or that to get a rooster to crow at set times you should feed him quartz crystals; and, most important of all, that rotating crops allows the sun to hit them on all four sides. So naturally, his angle on aesthetics differed from mine. I went down the canyon with him solely to observe his reaction.

Although not as spectacular as the Grand, Hell's Canyon is, in it's own sloping way, impressive. At its deepest point, as I watched my neighbor eyeing the geology, I couldn't help myself; I finally asked him what he thought.

He said, "Why, I'd sure like to roll a tire down from up there!"

DAY 9. Snowed. Dave tipped over and got his head wet today. As soon as he rolled up, he said, "To hell with this," and crawled out onto a raft. "Evolution," he explained from his new perch.

Upon reaching camp the Sloth lumbered ashore—lawn chair in tow—and began to read. He is now on page 1,386 halfway through the introduction. He had announced earlier that *Boise* is definitely Michener's finest work and that in a short while the earthworms will be evolving.

DAY 10. At camp (Bert Loper's port garboard strake), after the Sloth, Gan, and his woman retired from the aesthetic fire they didn't help build, the rest of us discussed the merits of Gan's woman, as follows:

REASONS FOR BRINGING RUBBER DUMMY

☞ Rubber Dummy does not eat.
☞ Rubber Dummy does not fill up rocket boxes.
☞ Rubber Dummy does not argue.
☞ Rubber Dummy stores easy in raft or can be blown up to add extra flotation.

REASONS AGAINST BRINGING RUBBER DUMMY

☞ Rubber Dummy cannot be nibbled on neck.
☞ Rubber Dummy can burst if left unattended in sun.
☞ Rubber Dummy is not Coast-Guard approved.

DAY 11. There is such an overload of history down here! Tonight we camped (binnacle sheets slept in by Bert Loper) where the famous first Briggs and Stratton National Geographic-sponsored expedition ended. This was the premier attempt to run the Grand Canyon on a kitchen table. Briggs and Stratton's try, however, failed when their center leaf broke, forcing them to walk out at this point. In a second expedition they succeeded, but having lost all their food they were forced to eat their film.[4]

DAY 12. Not all are enthusiastic about the canyon—for example,

---

4 Fortunately, nothing developed.

the Kaibab Squirrels. The canyon is regarded by these squirrels the same way the DMZ is in Korea. It is a barrier that has separated those on the north rim from those on the south rim for so long that many naturalists consider them to be two distinct species (the squirrels, not Koreans, although this may be happening to them, too). Sightings are now quite rare thanks to the earlier settlers who considered them a delicacy. Roasted on a skewer, they were known as "shish kaibab."

DAY 13. Camped at the figurehead of Bert Loper's boat. Snowing heavily. Although the water temperature released at the dam is 0 degrees centigrade here, thirteen days downstream, it has warmed up to a comfortable 32 degrees Fahrenheit. We argued over the value of switching over to the Julian Calendar, but decided not to since we couldn't conclude whether the two weeks difference would end the trip or start us all over again. We *were* positive, however, about who we would not bring another time—especially after today. The Sloth, sound asleep at the oars, flipped his raft in an insignificant rapid losing what remained of our beer. This evening, babbling nonsense about river gods, I decided that if he ever mentions such poppycock divinities again, I shall kill him.

DAY 14. This evening while we were camped (Bert Loper's shaft coupling) sentimentality overtook me as I observed the ideal picture of romance. A Maxfield Parrish-like sunset painted, shadowed, and highlighted the canyon walls while in the foreground Gan and his woman shared intimately in the wonders of tandem Nintendo. Unable to control myself, I crawled close enough to hear these two love birds chirping (anthropologists take note).

> Gan: It's the bomb!
> Rubber Dummy: Huh?
> Gan: Cool. You know?
> Rubber Dummy: Like rad?
> Gan: Yeah! Rad, like cool!

Once, in Turkey, I heard a young American trying to correct a Turkish girl who had just said, "Okey dokey doe."
"Not, okey dokey doe," the American explained. "That's hick."
"'Hick?' What is this 'hick?'"

"Not cool. You know?"

"Oh, yes, I know. Cool, it is like cold."

"No, no, cool, is like you're hot!"

"How can this be?"

"It's like bad."

"I don't understand."

"Bad is when you're really, really good."

"This does not make sense! You say something is cold, and it is hot. Then you say bad and it is good."

"That's right. When you're bad, you're good. You're hep."

"Hep? What is . . . Oh, I get so confused!"

"What do you say to starting over then?"

The girl sighed angelically, looked to the sky, and exclaimed, "Okey dokey doe."

DAY 15. Camped (poop deck, Bert Loper's head) where Bessie

Scouting Lava Falls. We ran it on the right.

supposedly shot her husband, Glen. Glen accused her of letting the bagels get wet. Despite the suspicious holes found in Glen there are serious holes in this shooting theory, since no guns are allowed in the Grand Canyon. I doubt there would be many river guides left if guns were allowed. Funny thing, how people can get on each other's nerves down here!

DAY 16. Lava Falls. Regulations stated that all articles about the Grand Canyon must mention the name. Dave made a cameo appearance in his kayak to run it, but he quickly reverted to the raft.

DAY 17. Years ago, I went down the canyon with the World's Greatest Rafter. How did I know he was the world's greatest? He told me so. He also told me and the group that we did not do anything right. His unmarked grave is just past mile 194. I'm sure he wouldn't have liked the way we communally strangled him, but it did the job.

DAY 18. At camp (Bert Loper's crow's-nest and rigging—two black balls were still in the rigging) I asked the Sloth if he ever planned to do any work on the trip. During the ensuing discussion I tried to emphasize my point with a frying pan but he countered my point with an oar . . .

DAY 1. October 15. Lee's Ferry, named after the Mormon scapegoat John D. Lee. Not seeing much future in wiping out wagon trains, Lee moved here to gouge the settlers in a new way, but in 1877 he was executed for overcharging on his ferry.

Reconfirmed the rumor that a constant flow of 25,000 cfs is false. This rumor was started the day after the dam was built and has been in circulation ever since.

All day I have forced myself not to wonder about some of the members of this group. However, this evening my attitude has shifted. Pulling into camp, one of our three rafters sent his girlfriend rushing into the bushes to claim the best real estate for their tent. In the meantime, this same rafter sat deeply immersed in thought while engaging in mortal combat on his pocket Nintendo. Another rafter simply unloaded a lawn chair (the only one on the trip) and a Michener book, Boise, sat down, and began to read while the rest of us unloaded his raft. With such suspect behavior starting already, I hope this trip will unfold into a good one. Somehow, I am struck with a strange sense of déjà vu.

INDIA

Fastly Down the Spiti

The canoe was as much mobbed in the train as in the water by visitors. At every station there was a crowd about the parcel van to see it; and often a whole train was emptied of passengers, who flocked from their carriages to look at the travelled kyak. But in England, too, these boats are novelties; and what think you was the name they were scheduled under, when two canoes came to a Midland station, and the head office was asked how they should be charged: Answer by telegram, "Charge them as invalid chairs—the double price of perambulators."

—John MacGregor, *The Rob Roy on the Baltic*, 1892

❖　❖　❖

I have sometimes imagined what the U.S. would be like if it had been the Hindus who had tried discovering a new route to Europe and had accidentally found America. Think of the possibilities! Instead of Plymouth Rock, these Hindu Pilgrims would have landed at Alcatraz. George "Ravi" Washington would have chopped down a Banyan tree. There would have been a period of Eastern expansion. "Go East, young man!" would have been the cry. And when the Civil War erupted, Abe "Mahatma" Lincoln would have freed the untouchables. Meanwhile, in the plains, great protests would have erupted over the "Red Europeans" killing and eating the sacred buffalo. This, of course, would have led to

◄ Andy, doing a nose stand with his feet. By flattening with a truck what remained of the previously broken-off bow, we bolted the break together, melted the seam—and gave the revised product, an "ampubat," to Carol.

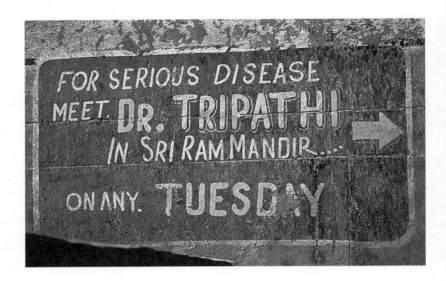

FOR SERIOUS DISEASE MEET DR. TRIPATHI IN SRI RAM MANDIR.... ON ANY. TUESDAY

the European Wars, producing sayings such as, "The only good European is a dead European." Eventually, the Europeans would all have been shipped to reservations, mostly to Oklahoma Pradesh, and the Indians could finally have advanced east unencumbered, paving the way for a strengthened nation and laying the eventual groundwork for the Atlantic Rim Economy. However, there would be downsides too. McDonald's franchises would be poor investments. And the sacred cow would have a devastating effect on the development of commerce, but at least the cows would make for some entertaining traffic jams . . . "Hi this is Don Juan, your Tex-Mex 'eye in the sky' reporter. If you're heading into Los Bramas from the west, expect some short delays, since there's a sacred shorthorn closing two lanes of the expressway. But if you're traveling from the east, expect long delays, since there's a herd of sacred longhorns blocking all lanes of traffic and it looks like them doggies were into some really green grass last night, making for slippery driving conditions. The state patrol is recommending chains or studded tires. Reporting for the Sacred K-O-W radio, where the bull is sacred, I'm Don Juan. . . . "

As for—

KAYAKING IN INDIA . . .

Before you go kayaking in India, there are certain things you should know about the country—facts you won't find here. The

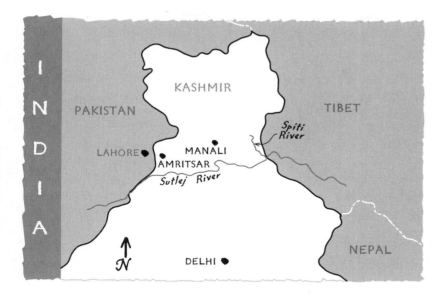

first thing I *can* tell you, though, is that all flights arrive in India in the middle of the night. There are specific reasons for this. For one thing, taxis can charge whatever they feel like when taking you to a hotel you don't want to go to, a hotel that also will charge you roughly the amount you will spend in the ensuing three months. But the foremost reason for night arrivals is that there is livestock on the runway in the day. Which brings up—

COWS . . .

Cows continue to be sacred in India, which is why hamburgers are made of soybeans, and that accounts for hamburger joints called *Wimpys*. The country harbors many species of cows. I myself discovered a new species in Varanasi. It had blue horns with red dots on them. When I attempted to photograph it, the cow tried to take me and I did what anyone would do who comes from where I do: I kicked it squarely in the head. And the gathering mob did what any mob would do coming from where they did: They picked up rocks and began to threaten me. Hastily I explained that, having lost my glasses, I had mistaken the cow for a being of no consequence, an old, crippled widow who had declined to throw herself on her husband's funeral pyre. The crowd quickly apologized and I walked away unscathed. This brings up cremations.

There are many cremations along the banks of the Ganges. These are done at burning ghats—an acronym for General Hysterical Agreement for Trade. Ghat insures free trade between wood and bodies at fixed prices, making everyone in Geneva happy. It is here (the Ganges, not Geneva) where the dogs sit and warm themselves by these fires and, whenever hungry, snatch morsels from the fire—a belly button, a duodenum, a gaskin, an extensor digitorum longus, a post-nasal drip, or some such barbecued tidbit. I didn't like the dogs; they seemed to be regarding me with special interest as they discussed, then argued, among themselves (mostly at night under my hotel window) how another nationality might taste.

A favorite place to be cremated is in Varanasi, and dead people come from all over India to do so. It is also Varanasi where thousands come to bathe in the Ganges—although "to bathe" is a contradiction in terms, because by the time the Ganges reaches Varanasi, it is a festering sewer. This brings up at last—

Varanasi, where corruption is widespread, seating is at a premium, and hygiene is unheard of.

KAYAKING . . .

Do not kayak here. Anyway, the Ganges at Varanasi is very holy. It is also very nasty. Upon seeing the river, many pilgrims are so overcome with joy they run and jump in the river and then, remembering they can't swim, drown. Others who *can* swim, jump in, contract one of sixty-seven fatal diseases, and die. It is a good idea to make cremation arrangements ahead of time.

We—Carol and I—quickly left Varanasi, which brings up—

TRAVELING IN INDIA . . .

Basically, there are three ways to go. By "Tata," "tuk-tuk," or "choo-choo." That's how it is in third-world countries . . . . I suppose this categorization has just annoyed someone, but really, I'm not shooting from the hip. India *is* third world, as it fits neatly into one of my many generalizations, specifically rule #49, which states: Countries which drive on the left are *third world*. Countries that drive down the middle of the road are *developing*, and countries that don't drive anymore are called *Haiti*. And my categories continue. To help you understand India, I'll break down its population into occupations. Thus:

Human Groups
Taxi drivers 45%
Rickshaw drivers 23%
Money changers 19%
Holy people 16%
People who think they are
    holy people but aren't 15%
Beggars 13%
Boat owners in Varanasi 11%
House boat owners in Kashmir . 11%
General nuisances 10%
Subhuman groups
Police 24%
Army 18%
**Subtotal of subhuman
groups divided by 2** 29%
Total 192%

Ha! I hear you laugh! There's no such thing as 192%! Oh, *yeah*? Well, that's why India is so overcrowded![1] If you're still in doubt, try boarding any public bus (Tata), where human molecular fusion is an everyday occurrence. And it was on such a Tata that Carol and I traveled north to Manali to meet kayaking physician, Andy Watt.

I asked a local, "How do you find Dr. Watt?"

The local replied, "He's got a horrible sense of humor."

"Can you give me an example?" I asked.

"He claims that with the combination of kayaking and dysentery, squirt boating originated in Manali."

"You're right. If I were writing an article, I would never say that."

In time we found Andy who led us to his room. Upon entering, I smashed my head on the door, thus enrolling in a crash course in astronomy. When I regained consciousness, Andy was examining an X-ray of my dented skull.

"Incredible," he said. "There's no brain." Then he disappeared into the bathroom and, lying in the tub, continued to peruse my X-ray. Suddenly he leapt up and ran out the door, naked, yelling, "Eureka! I've found it!"

When the police returned him, he was still wild with excitement. He showed me the X-ray. "Here. This spec here. I thought it was a dust spot, but really, it's your brain. Immature. Childish at best. All this other area: wasted space!"

It wasn't easy for Andy, being a doctor in Manali. Like Mother Teresa, Andy gave of himself completely, descending remote and perilous rivers to heal the poor. But through all his years of such service, the Nobel prize committee has steadily overlooked his efforts because he has refused to wear a nun's habit.

"Surely," I said, "you could tell them about your other bad ones." But my suggestion fell on deaf ears.

One day I watched Andy work and marveled at the multitude of people he treated; his waiting room looked like a circus recruiting new talent. There were Swamis, Punjabis, Tibetans, and Yogis. There were also freaks, who had parked themselves in Manali, the end the hippie trail. When not frying themselves on drugs they sat around and practiced their yogurt. At best, they dressed with a pajama party in mind, like, say, *Beach, Blanket, Barbiturates*. Their clothes, hanging off them like drapes, were tailored with an ele-

---

[1] Projecting from India's current population growth, by the year 2146 there will be one person per every square foot of country. Fortunately, by that time, given the advances in science and technology, every person should be able to own their own boombox.

phant in mind, and their color scheme suggested material tie-dyed in a factory run by lunatics. One such patient, there to see Andy, asked, "My mum doesn't want me taking any Indian medicine for my giardia, so she sent this Tiniba from England. What are the complications if I take it with acid?"

The other difficulty for Andy in Manali was that Gerry Moffat and Guy Robbins had moved into town. They were playing the parts of Sean Connery and Michael Cain in *The Man Who Would Be King*, only Gerry and Guy were building their empire through a rafting business. They asked Andy to run safety boat, promising to pay him—but only if he finished the run. So far, Andy had completed one out of five runs. Often raft customers would ask, "Hey! Where's the safety boater?" To which the reply came, "He's back upstream scouting a drop. If you see his paddle or boat float by, could you tell us so we can pick them up?"

One day Gerry asked if I wanted to be safety boat.

"Gerry," I said, "believe it or not, there is life after thirty, and as it appears now there may even be life after forty, I intend to enjoy it and not cut it short. That which you are referring to as Grade 5, we used to consider a Grade 67 minus. The Grade 4 I refer to is what you now refer to as a Grade 2 minus. In the old days, when *we* ran rivers, if someone was so foolish as to run a Grade 5, we would—if he survived—ostracize him, break his fingers, and commit him to a mental institution. And if he ever escaped and called us, we left specific instructions with our mothers, wives, or girlfriends to tell him we were not at home. And if we were unfortunate enough to answer the phone ourselves, we insisted he had a wrong number and hung up. I have continued to employ this policy and it looks now that, as long as I'm not shot by anyone who hates my articles, I shall live to see fifty."

Speaking of guns, Gerry then told me a story involving a shotgun, a father, and a recent Iranian girlfriend, but I digress . . . .

All this while we had been waiting, day after day, for a bus to the Tsarp-cum-Zanskar, a river that is hard at low water, difficult in a large runoff, and extremely hard in winter. In fact, the Zanskar is so hard in winter that the locals walk on it to replenish their supply of Arrak when they run short. Each day Andy would go to the bus station, asking about a bus and demanding an evasive answer. Finally, one morning we simply left: We fought our way onto a bus. (Don't let me over-emphasize how crowded these buses are. Really, they are no problem to get on just so long as you tape your ears for the scrum at the door.) We headed—not to the Tsarp, because the bus wasn't going there—but to the Spiti, a river we knew nothing about.

Wherever the road wasn't washed or avalanched away was crooked as a tub of guts; it climbed up and down the sides of mountains in such a fanatical, irresponsible way that I wished there was more grime on the windows to keep me from temporarily abandoning my atheist leanings. I began imagining our kayaks and gear shaking loose from the rack and disappearing irretrievably down some abyss. I also began imagining the bus plunging into the same abyss. But I found consolation in the fact that when they recovered the pieces of my body, my femur and tibia would be permanently welded at the knee, thanks to the Tata's legroom, which was adequate for a busload of two-year-olds.

Indian Tata buses require a dynamic duo to operate them. Besides actually driving, Tata drivers are also easily identifiable by their Sid Vicious haircuts and their smoldering, serial-killer stares. Their partners, the conductors, are an even lesser species who parrot only two words: "Chello," which they chant to the driver to let him know the left front wheel is still on the road; and "AHHHH-HHHHH!" which lets the driver know he has just driven over a cliff.

On the bus I had little time to enjoy the scenery, since all the passengers wished to know my opinion on the philosophical aspects of Heisenberg's Uncertainty Principle.

"What is your name?" A passenger asked. I replied and asked his name.

"Thank you, thank you," he said.

"You're welcome. Where are you going, Thank you, Thank you?" I asked.

"Thank you, thank you," he said.

"You're welcome. Are you married Thank you, Thank you?"

"Thank you, thank you."

"You're welcome. Children?"

"Thank you, thank you."

Passing some snow-covered peaks, Thank you, Thank you swept his hand toward the sight, anxious that I not miss it. "*Barf*," he said, his eyes misting with tears.

"Andy?"

"Aye?"

"Yes, you. What's *barf* mean?"

"Snow."

A short while later, Thank you, Thank you turned green, and even a shorter while later the following conversation took place: "Andy?"

"Aye?"

"Yes, you. It just snowed on my leg."

Fortunately, I was soothed by the surround-sound music on the bus. To the uneducated Western ear, this music seems primitive, but after intense study during numerous bus rides I came to realize that the Herculean effort the Indians use to deflect, curve, hang, deform, and corrupt their notes makes Bing Crosby look like a thirty-pound weakling. Unlike Western music, Indian music is designed and enhanced to be played through dragging tape decks and crummy speakers. What I didn't realize is that it is also designed to be listened to on a minimum of six aspirin. But I digress once more. I am trying to get to—

KAYAKING . . .

A born interviewer, the next person I sat with probed me with the intensity of a Spanish Inquisition. I gave him my name, my country, my zip and area codes, the number of kids I don't have, my sister's name, my brother's name, and on and on, until at last, once I had passed the oral exam, he asked me for my address. I got up and moved but it was no use. The bus ride was twelve hours long and I endured fourteen more interviews, until I could no longer stand it. At last I sat next to a Kashmiri and, like most Kashmiris, he was insidiously conniving, a pathological liar, hopelessly lazy, and terminally cynical. We had a lot in common. He asked me my name.

"Jimmy Hoffa," I replied. "Some people think I'm hiding in hot dogs, but it's not true."

"What is your country?"

"Freeloadia. Gateway to the Philander Isles. Right next to the Diminutive Republic."

"Do you have children?"

"Yes, I did—twenty-five of them, in fact, but since I'm an advocate of retroactive abortion, I disposed of the lot of them. I caught them listening to rap. Don't get me wrong, there should be exceptions for child prodigies, like Mozart. Did you know that he wrote Beethoven's Fifth Symphony when he was only five years old?"

"How many brothers do you have?"

"Two, both tragic stories. One fell in love with a woman with multiple personalities. It was one of the worst love triangles you've ever seen—until he developed a split personality of his own. After that he went on double dates with his girlfriend. Meantime he worked in the molasses business, but he was always being fired for having sticky fingers. That and he was short. Because he was only four foot twelve he was constantly being overlooked for promotions. Eventually, though, he became a C.E.O. but soon after was shot in a hostile takeover bid.

"My other brother worked at the United Nations, but unfortunately, he was xenophobic. He checked everyone's weapons in at the front door. They called him a piece keeper. After he was let go he went into raising water buffaloes, but all his sea horses went lame on him. Please, I can't continue."

"How many sisters do you have?"

"I had one of them, too, but she's no more. She was a Jain— a strict vegetarian, like me. Couldn't stand to see anything killed that had a face. But she kept putting ketchup on her steaks. I went gaga. Really, I don't know what came over me. I used an axe. Bullets are so expensive these days."

In time, we arrived in the Spiti valley, an arid, rock-intense land of geology run amuck. If you want to know what both India and Pakistan will look like after they nuke each other into oblivion, visit Spiti. It's on the southwest corner of the Tibetan plateau, a place that prior to history was pristine seashore, where Tibetans did nothing but wander up and down the beach picking up sea shells to incorporate into their handicrafts and sell to tourists. Then came India. Fed up with apartheid, it broke away from South Africa and went looking for a happier existence, but unfortunately the navigator was drunk and India slammed into Tibet with the velocity of a speeding Tata. The impact registered off the Richter scale, but fortunately everyone was wearing seat belts and there were few injuries. The land is still smoking from the collision.

As for the culture, the area was untainted. We were among the first Westerners in several decades to exploit the valley. A small child in traditional dress approached us. Here was a picture of innocence. Tears filled my eyes at the sight. The child held out his hand. "Bon bon?" he asked.

Andy took the child's hand and shook it. "Not Bon Bon. Andy Watt." Then Andy explained to us the story of that French scoundrel, Phillipe Bonaparte, Napoleon's great-great-grandson, or, as he was better known, "Bon Bon." Bon Bon was the first explorer in this region, and he came without provisions. Instead he lived off the people, promising them great things when he returned. Of course, he never came back, but everyone now asks each Westerner hopefully, "Bon Bon?"

We viewed what was supposed to be our river. I mean it looked *almost* like a river and had all the necessary ingredients for a river. All it lacked was one detail. Disappointment stained Andy's face.

"It's unrun," I reminded him.

"Because there's no water."

"Look at the bright side."

"What?"

"I don't know."

Eventually we found water in a small gorge containing a crowd of boulders and some bona fide eddies. Before entering the gorge, and assuming the roar of water would drown out voice communication, we—keeping with the Indian motif—decided on several visual signals:

The u-joint nod

MEANING: Yes it can be run, and no it can't be run, by which I mean perhaps in the monsoon when the huge hole that can't be avoided is flooded over, or, when the river is lower than it is presently, like in winter when that hole might turn into an eddy, but at this level definitely maybe by which I also mean I would run it if I felt I had the talent while remembering, however, that if I messed up and Shiva, God of Destruction, saw to it that I went into that hole, well . . . maybe it actually could still be run if I could hold my breath for a quarter of an hour. OK?

The hand twist

MEANING: Well, yes, his run was going well until he dropped into that huge hole, and no one has seen him for at least a quarter of an hour.

But fortunately, there was no need for signals. With sub-zero temperatures and a 110 m.p.h. wind blowing sand upriver, the effect of the whitewater was lost on us. Instead, this gorge seemed to contain the combined disadvantages of a Himalayan winter and a Gobi Desert sandstorm. Nevertheless, I tried capturing on film the fact that there was whitewater here, only to discover that where my hands used to be was now something inanimate and extremely cold—a condition I could only correct with a large bonfire. This brought up another problem: There was no wood. We knew, however, that the locals used yak dung for fuel. It took us two hours just to capture a yak, then two more hours waiting for it to comply with our wishes—and, when the time came, Andy became excited and accidentally set the animal's tail on fire. It was two more hours before our tailless yak lost interest in flattening our camp and finally, after his revenge was complete, he wandered off.

On the third day, the river still continued its grade 1 character, except where we took a wrong channel; then we had to walk. We came to a monastery that looked like a beehive, parked our boats, and climbed up to it. Even from a distance we could hear the "punga," the monks chanting in harmonic monotones, "Onepen onepen onepen onepen onepen onepen." Upon entering the building I smashed my head on the door jam. When I regained consciousness a monk was reciting prayers for me, soothing my headache, backing up his vocals with drum and symbol. I wallowed

Monastery near Spiti, where a monk soothes my headache with his drumming.

in sadness; I would never have strayed from Catholicism had I been given such a drum set with which to chant my prayers: *Dominatrix Nabisco* BASH!

After being given several gallons of tea we were introduced to the head monk and his wife, who was apparently one of the perks of the job; all the underlings are celibate. From beneath his robe he produced a fossil and passing it to us asking, "Want to buy?"

Shaking our heads we handed it back.

"How about carpets? I have very old carpets to sell."

"I'll bet you do, but no thanks," I said.

"Buddhas? I have lots of Buddhas."

"No," Andy answered decisively.

With this he left the room but soon returned with my sleeping bag. "How about this?"

"That's my sleeping bag!"

"Very old."

"It just smells that way, now give it back!" I demanded, grabbing it from him.

"That'll be one thousand rupees."

"I don't have one thousand rupees and besides it's *mine*."

"We take VISA."

After retrieving what had been pillaged from our boats we at last escaped the monastery and, deviating from our plans, took a small hike that involved a local trader, a horse, and a low communal intelligence on our part to leave the river, for this actually meant exercise. We hiked into an area never taken advantage of by Westerners, and after several hours of climbing I could see why. I tried to be optimistic. "Sure is no air pollution up here," I said.

"That's 'cause there's no air," Andy replied.

Soon we came to a village where people asked about our occupations.

"If I tell them we'll be here all day," Andy said.

"Give me five bucks or I'll tell them."

We were there all day. I only went along on one house call. The patient was in a dark corner of a dark room. Andy began asking dark questions.

"Vomiting?"

"Yes," I answered.

"How long ago?" he asked the patient.

"About two hours ago," I replied again.

"And how do *you* know all this?" Andy finally asked me.

"You come sit here and put your hand where I just did."

Andy regarded the patient once more and said to me, "TB or not TB. That's the question. I'd wash my hands if I were you."

The next day's trek climbed straight up until at last we were at the top of a huge pass where we were buffeted by what seemed like ceaseless winds. Andy asked our guide if the wind always blew that way.

"No," he replied. "The rest of the time it blows the other way."

Despite the present hurricane, the pass afforded a fantastic panorama of mountains. Looking down I commented, "That's a great view of Mount Everest."

"You're a darn fool," said Andy. "*That's* not Everest. *That's* K2! Everest is down there!"

Just over the pass we were forced to camp. Our trader-guide told us that it was *dry* yak dung we were supposed to burn, so we set off to collect the night's cooking fuel, and in several hours we had half a cord. This was stacked in a neat pile by the fire next to the neat pile of icicles which Carol had been collecting from an icefall. But as it grew dark the water and the fuel integrated, and only by pretending that the melted ice had been spiced with dill could we drink it.

That night the temperature dropped to 35 degrees below absolute zero. But my worst problem was a splitting headache, and I awoke Andy to let him know.

"Andy?"

"Aye?"

"Yes, you. I've got a splitting headache."

"You've come down with altitude sickness," he said.

"Nonsense! I've been coming up all day, at least twenty thousand feet this afternoon alone."

"Hmmmm. Good point. I'll notify the medical journals immediately. I can see it now. Dr. Watt discovers that people come *up* with altitude sickness . . . "

"OK, OK! I've come *up* with it. What's the cure?"

"A splitting headache? The left hemisphere has separated from the right. Which means . . . you're only in your right mind! Ha ha ha."

"Please Andy, I'm close to death. What does it mean?"

"There's nothing left! Ha ha ha. Here, suck on this for five minutes."

"A *quinine tablet?*"

"Yes."

"Will it help?"

"No, but it'll keep you from waking me in the middle of the night."

The next day we hiked towards Tibet, turned around, and climbed the pass once more. At the end of the hike, Andy returned to Manali, but not before teaching me some Hindi—at least what I *assumed* was Hindi. I prided myself on being the only American who could speak Hindi with a Scottish accent. But really, in my innocence, I was the victim of a cruel and warped joke. One day, while out hiking, Carol and I arrived in a village: cold, hungry, destitute, and with nowhere to cash an American Express traveler's check. There were no hotels, restaurants, or anyone who could speak English to help us. At last I had to rely on Andy's teachings.

Me (thinking I am asking for a room for the night): "Hello! My name is Ross Cromarty and I've just taken the high road and my haggis is suffering from stomach trouble, my sporran has gone completely limp, my tattoos have all washed off, my tam-o'-shanter blew away, and now all my marbles are rolling out."

Hotel owner (eyeing me with the same gaze I would apply to Christmas carolers showing up at my doorstep in summer): "Yes."

Me (believing now that I am offering him a price for the room): "You see, I've just tossed seventeen capers and my bagpipes are winded, and if it weren't for the bees swarming in them there'd be no drones at all. You'd know what I mean, if you'd ever been roamin' in the gloamin' with a lassie and a flaccid claymore."

Hotel owner (calling to his wife so that she won't miss this): "WILMA!"

Me (now thinking that I am now asking for food): "Really, you won't believe it, but I've forgotten all my old acquaintances and even my donkeys have lost their bon bonny braes."

At which point the hotel owner sicked his yak on us.

As for the rest of the trip, there is nothing more to tell, because several nights later we attended a dance called the lobotomy limbo in a village of short people. After much arrak I was coaxed to join in. The steps went: two forward, one back. Two forward, one back. Two forward—and it was then that I encountered:

A LOW BEAM.

Art deco Miami Beach, where a hundred dollars buys the same cockroach-infested room that three bucks fetch in New Delhi. Besides that, English is spoken in New Delhi.

EVERGLADES

Uphill in a Swamp

To the jubilant surprise of Palm Beach, Whit Deschner (cum laude dadee da) self-made fool, made a cameo appearance in town this week, with the intention of onward travel into the Everglades. Arriving this time with a small entourage, he only rented three floors of the famous Breakers Hotel. Again, Deschner, did not arrive on his yacht the M/V Mine's Bigger Than Yours. *He has in the past strongly criticized the Army Corps of Engineers for not dredging the inland waterway to accommodate his yacht's draft. However, this time, upon hearing of Deschner's arrival, Donald Trump immediately put his yacht and his wine at Deschner's disposal. Both were quickly disposed of. Salvage crews expect to refloat Trump's yacht sometime next week. . . .*

—Palm Beach Post-Herald

◆　◆　◆

Ha ha. Just kidding. Actually, it was Carol who, amid a procession of the whining rich in their purring Rolls Royces, BMWs, Mercedes, Jaguars, and expensive little bubble cars, picked me up at the West Palm Beach Airport in our rattling Isuzu Diesel.

The February temperature had dipped to a chilly 50 degrees and the locals were complaining. They had to put the tops up on their convertibles, turn off the air conditioning, and put clothes on. In Florida, freeze has nothing to do with temperature. Say the word indiscriminately around shady strangers, and you can find yourself ventilated with bullets. Of course, living in such a temperate climate isn't without hazards. In 1992 lower Florida was economically devastated when Hurricane Andrew blew over approximately two-and-a-half billion dollars' worth of billboards advertising airboat rides through the Everglades.

The first thing noticeable about Florida is that it would be a good headquarters for the Flat Earth Society. Climb onto the roof of any high-rise and you can see across the state; it is, supposedly, a peninsula, but it is really a big, long sand spit with a backyard swamp. Florida has fewer mountain-climbing casualties than any other state in the nation.

It was Ponce de Leon who, covered with Spanish flies, discovered this terra-but-questionable-firma. Ironically, in a place that now boasts more Geritol sales than anywhere else in the world, he had come sniffing for the Fountain of Youth. Ponce, of course, failed in his mission, and what he mistakenly discovered and thought to be the Fountain of Youth was really the Fountain of Immaturity. For this blunder, he and his men paid dearly. To the end of their short-lived, puerile lives, they constantly fooled one another with rubber snakes, squirting flowers, fake dog poop, and poo poo cushions. Attempting to make peace with the local Indians, Ponce secured the deal with a handshake—along with a hidden buzzer—and his men were immediately dispatched.

After Ponce, Florida was shuffled more or less unwanted between nations, until the Miami Dolphins at last bought it in the later half of the 1900s. Unfortunately, their first few home games were marred by swarms of mosquitoes from the nearby Everglades. If the mosquitoes had maintained self-discipline and ignored this new source of junk food, then no one would ever have attempted draining the Everglades. Today, although conservation efforts have slowed the process, the developers (solely for the well-being of mankind) now have their sights set on draining the Gulf of Mexico to make room for more hamburger and sport franchises, and the occasional golf course. Besides, the lately retired, freshly deceased make a terrific landfill.

In West Palm Beach, I was handed my first big disappointment in life. Somehow, I'd imagined the area to be more rural, like a two-lane windy road between palm trees and citrus orchards, not I-95 snaking between high-rises. The palm trees were there all right, but the neighborhood does not derive its name from them; it comes from all the palm readers. West Palm is plagued with drug problems, unlike nearby Palm Beach, where residents such as the Kennedys made their respectable millions through bootlegging. West Palm is beachless, while Westless Palm Beach has a beach and it goes to great lengths to keep the residents of West Palm away from it. So the residents of West Palm merely shrug and say "fine, keep your beach and you can have Hurricane Whit, too," the impending storm of the millennium that will reduce all high-class rabble to low-grade rubble. I'm sorry, but there's something morally amuck about a place that devotes entire rows in supermarkets to Martini olives.

Nowhere else have I ever seen such an eye-opening division between the classes. For example, while I was there an incident occurred demonstrating just how ever-widening this gap is: A small executive aircraft, losing power, tried for an emergency landing on a golf course, but the golfers refused to budge, and the pilot, swerving to avoid them, clipped a palm tree and totaled the plane. Rioting between golfers and pilots was imminent.

Driving south, we came to hurricane-bait Miami. It was tough to tell where West Palm stopped and Miami started, let alone identify what might constitute Fort Lauderdale in between. Freeway exits were well-marked with plenty of warning—right up to the one before ours. On ours, however, three more inside lanes had been secretly added, and no warning was given for our exit. The fact that we successfully made a 90-degree turn at 70 m.p.h. and traversed three lanes of traffic was a large miracle. But the next requirement was a twenty-five-millisecond decision between going north or west, when we wanted neither. Of course, we picked the greater of these two evils, a turn that quickly landed us in what obviously was Havana, because everyone was suddenly speaking Spanish. I'd never thought of Havana as being north or west of Miami, but nevertheless, there it was.

By taking every available wrong turn, we at last came to Miami Beach, a place where everyone is welcome, providing they can find a parking place. The car-to-parking-space ratio is roughly 2000 to 1. Here we wandered through the art deco district, renting, for a hundred bucks, an art deco room in an art deco hotel. Three bucks fetches the same thing in Delhi. The room was clean but the maid, obviously feeling sentimental, had left a previous occupant's message written—in lipstick—on the mirror. Surrounded by a big heart, it read:

"John, You were the greatest last night. Love Bob."

All night we were bitten by art deco bedbugs, while listening to art deco sex through extremely thin art deco walls. It was just a taste of the fast, furious life of the region, and as I lay there enjoying the art deco neon flashing through the curtainless window, I consoled myself with the fact that at least crocodiles are making a comeback in the cooling waters of the nuclear power plant that lights up Miami.

In time we arrived in the Everglades, an even flatter place than the rest of Florida, due to its lack of buildings. The Everglades is not a swamp at all but a river, fifty miles wide and dropping a dizzying *two inches per mile*. It is not a place where you just pull over to the bank for lunch.

Anyone who steps off the road automatically relinquishes all priority on the food chain. Alligators were everywhere, along with the occasional three-headed, radiation-mutated crocodile. Signs adamantly warned:

DO NOT FEED THE ANIMALS.
DO NOT DISTURB THE WILDLIFE.

Yet they didn't say what to do if an alligator is gnawing off your leg, which would be a simultaneous but contradictory violation of both rules. Perhaps it was the same author who, on park literature, advised staying out of the sun—then because of insects, recommended avoiding shade also.

I should have posed these paradoxes to the ranger at the Visitor Center, because he was a know-it-all Easterner. Checking in to reserve campsites for the epic trip we were about to embark on, we told him of our intention to paddle up the coast then circle back through the park interior. The ranger said, "Now, if you're starting up the coast, you'll want to be aware of the tides here. They can really affect your progress."

"How big are they?" I asked.

"Two feet."

"*Two feet!* You call that a tide? Listen, I've been on fishing

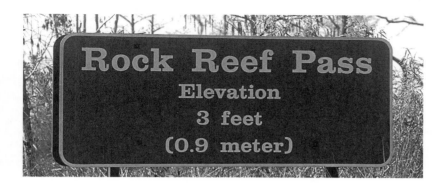

Rock Reef Pass
Elevation
3 feet
(0.9 meter)

High point of our trip.

boats in Alaska where I've encountered thirty-two-foot tides, and that was just the flood alone."

The ranger regarded me a short piece then continued. "Now most people do this trip in the opposite direction due to the prevailing breeze."

"Breeze? How strong is it?"

"Oh, nothing much; five, maybe ten miles an hour."

"And you call that a breeze! Why, in Alaska we call nothing under seventy miles an hour a breeze!"

"Huh, well, that might be, but I'm just saying, you might want to reconsider. Now then, you'll be entering the Joe River . . . "

" . . . River? There's a river there?"

"Well, yes, that's what your itinerary indicates. And your route shows you'll be going *up* it, whereas most people choose to come *down* it."

"How much of a drop are we talking about?"

"Well it doesn't really drop, but there can be a flow to it at times and . . . "

"Never mind the trifles. I'll tell, you I've paddled all over the world and I'm not about to concern myself about some languid little piece of backwater."

"Well," said the ranger, regarding me once more with bridged eyebrows, "I'd just like to say I told you."

Heading out in our canoe, Carol asked, "What do you think the tide's doing?"

"Does it matter?"

"What about these channel markers?"

"Never mind them, those are for boats. We'll just cut across here." Which we did, and promptly began to bump the bottom.

237

"Shall we turn around?"

"Naw, let's just keep going. All we need is the dew on the grass."

"Yes, but there is no grass."

We bumped bottom more frequently and Carol said, "I really do think we should turn around."

At which point, directly in front of the Ranger Station, we ran aground.

"Shall we get out and tow?"

"No. Let's have lunch."

A tour boat passed down the channel and hailed us. "Ahoy there!" The skipper shouted as hundreds of video cameras began recording this historic moment.

"Ahoy yourself!" I shouted back.

"What are you doing?"

"Having lunch. What's it look like?"

"I thought you might be stuck."

Two hours later the tour boat passed back up the channel. Over the loud speaker we heard, "Yep, they're still there. Looks like a long lunch break, folks."

In time the tide returned, and we began to paddle through the turquoise-brown waters, around several keys, across several banks. None of the keys fit the banks. A breeze came up and soon we were struggling against both wind and tide. I said, "Good thing because if we had the wind against the tide right now we could have some pretty rough water. Carol said something about how it was a good thing I knew everything, as otherwise she'd be in the dark. But even with all I knew, we arrived at our beach in the dark anyway. We slept well and, save for the occasional drug flight passing over, all was quiet.

The next day we rounded Cape Sable ("fifty-three days out, two masts broke but not before three men fell to their deaths. Two more crew washed overboard, the captain remained drunk while the rest suffered hideously from scurvy . . . ") and camped. Not that the rounding was fatiguing work, but the weather was nice, *so* nice that we spent an extra day on the beach, which proved our undoing. The following day, the ten m.p.h. breeze was blowing a good twenty right from the direction we had intended to paddle.

So we spent the day walking the beach, collecting sea shells. But these were hardly adequate, so I wandered into the mangroves and found an alligator head. Carol said, "What do you think the

Size 7 quadruple W footwear; "Two glade shoes."

Tibetans would trade us for all these shells?"

"Not half as much as they'd give me for this alligator head."

Carol sat admiring her Tibetan wealth; I admired my head. Then we gazed out at the keys, speculated which one was Gilligan's Island, and began recalling all the tragedies that had befallen them.

I said, "Did Gilligan ever find an alligator head?"

"I don't think so. What are you going to do with it?"

"Don't know. What do you think the alligator did with it?"

"Eat, but I'll bet he wouldn't have eaten you."

"Why not?"

"He'd have found you in bad taste. Besides, it would be such a waste of knowledge."

The next day the wind continued to blow, so we turned around and ventured into the marsh where the mangrove roots looked like pipe organs on acid. Besides crocodiles and alligators, the area is rich in birdlife. Whether they wish to be or not, all birds in Florida are migratory. Blown airborne in hurricanes they land in Florida's two adjoining states, New York and New Jersey. On my rare bird list I was able to check off: a scarlet-billed ibid., a great blue herring, a double-breasted carbuncle, a common egress, a fork-tailed spoonbill, and a four-winged plover. There were more ordinary species as well, like the royal tern, and as soon as I identified their flock I began heaving rocks at them.

"What are you doing!" Carol asked.

"Leaving no tern unstoned."

Prototype water-driven Ferris wheel on the lower Owyhee. The project was abandoned after several drownings. Because the Air Force keeps bombing it, the area is one of the least densely populated spots in the lower 48 states.

THE HIGH DESERT

Vacationing in Owyhee

Part of this pleasure flows from the mere sense of rapid motion. In going down a swift reach of river there is the same sensation about one's midriff that is felt when one goes forward smoothly on a lofty rope swing. Now the first few days on the Danube are upon very fast waters. Between its source and Ulm the descent of the river is about 1500 feet. This would give 300 feet of fall for each of a five day's journey; and therefore the prospect for the day's voyage is most cheering when you lunch in the morning and know that you will have to descend about as much as the height inside the dome of St. Paul's before you reach a halting for the night.

—John MacGregor, A Thousand Miles in the Rob Roy Canoe. 1881

◆　　◆　　◆

Located in northern Nevada, southwestern Idaho, and southeastern Oregon, the Owyhee country is a hunk of the remotest land left in the lower 48 states. To drive from one side of it to the other, a person had better be prepared not to see a McDonald's for an *entire* day. The area which consists of high, sparsely populated desert, is accessible only by kayak, horse, four-wheel drive, and, as a favorite target area for the Air Force, fighter jet. The name, Owhyee, derives from some Hawaiian guides lost in the Owhyee neighborhood in the last century. Having strayed all the way from Hawaii, they were as lost as you can get. Because of the name, today Hawaii and Owyhee are constantly confused with one another, which explains why so many kayakers mistakenly wind up in Hawaii. The two places have so much in common.

My first encounter with the Owyhee happened while I was busy sliding out of college, a situation accelerated by—in the middle of final's week—an invitation to go on a self-supported, week-long trip down the lower section of the Owyhee (from Rome to Jordan Valley—keeping in tune with Hawaiian place names). I could squeak by all my courses with a passing grade while missing the final—except for one class, Sociology. Thanks to extended kayaking excursions into Idaho, I'd already skipped a number of critical tests. I'd used the excuse of an extremely sick family that had various illnesses culminating, naturally, with my mom's funeral (the Lochsa River). But now I'd run out of credible excuses. Mistakenly, I tried what I reckoned to be a novel concept: honesty. For this, I was handed an immediate and decisive "F." I assured myself that I had learned at least one valuable lesson in college: Never tell the truth.

But that wasn't all. Over the ensuing week—and subsequent trips down this river—I observed more about sociology and life in general than I could have gleaned in a lifetime of listening to silly lectures. Diligently, I began jotting notes.

There were eight on that first trip: four bachelors and two married couples. At the put-in we all behaved like normal human beings; that is, the married couples spoke to the bachelors, and the bachelors replied without any visible trace of mockery. In fact, the discussion concerned a mutual agreement that since the weather was so hot—somewhere in the 90s—there was no need for wet-suits.

It was the temperature that gave us, the bachelors, our first clue that the goal posts for the trip had been moved. Wife faction of couple #1 said, "It's too hot to kayak."

"*Too hot to kayak?*" whispered one of my fellow bachelors, incredulously. "*That's* an impossibility."

Then wife #1 began to bitch about packing.

We bachelors began hoisting eyebrows at one another, and the following hushed conversation took place:

"She's the Wicked Witch."

"From which direction?"

"From *all points* of the compass."

Nevertheless, this small problem aside, the trip progressed well the first day, save for Spud. Spud belonged to married faction #2. Not only was Spud an unwilling participant who hated kayaking, he was also the unwilling skipper of a large freighter, which was now under way after being longshored by his wife, Elma. Some of the lighter items with which Elma had ballasted his boat were a cast-iron skillet and a cast-iron Dutch oven. She carried important things like their two pillows which, after she haphazardly loaded them, filled her boat. Spud's load was augmented regularly by rocks his wife busily collected. As a result, when Spud was right side up, he looked more like a submarine trying to surface. Thanks to his wife, he had become the world's first squirt boater. However, even if this fact had on dawned him, I doubt his words of exclamation would have changed. Fortunately, they were masked by large incoming quantities of water.

During the week we spent descending the river, Spud spent more time out of his boat than he did in it. He and his wife provided the Owyhee with enough flotsam to keep a beachcomber content for a lifetime. Each time we gathered up Spud and his wreckage, he became increasingly irritated. For reasons I still don't understand he took it all out on us, the bachelors. Well . . . maybe I do know, just a little.

Every time Spud took a dunk, Elma would ask, "Why'd you tip over, Spud?"

Of course, all four of us bachelors then wanted to know the

same thing, but Spud refused to answer. Still, we kept asking, at lunch, at dinner, at night, first thing in the morning, at breakfast, at each subsequent tipover, at lunch once more, and so on until Spud's face took on the look of a very disturbed person—a sociopath, in fact.

This behavior didn't go unnoticed by married couple #1, and on the following day All Points suddenly wanted to know why we didn't mind our own business.

"Because he's got the alcohol and we're worried about its safety," came the reply.

Then something truly bizarre happened. Elma demanded what business it was of All Points to be demanding of us what business it was of ours? We, of course, demanded what business it was of Elma's to demand what business it was of All Points to demand what business it was of ours. These certainly were not problems ever presented in sociology.

We experienced a brief detente until that night, when it was our turn, the bachelors, to fix dinner. Now our idea of an adequate meal would have been chips and beer, but the women, who had planned the menus, made us fix some fancy dishes they'd seen on the backs of cereal boxes. They had names like "pâté of corn flake and pineapple kebab," and "teriyaki béarnaise sauce with Fruit Loops on oysters," and "cacciatore-souffléed Rice Krispie tuna balls." It seemed like a lot of work until we discovered the après-dinner drinks. Wanting to know if such liquid was suitable for human consumption, we began testing it while preparing dinner. Things would have been fine except that, while preparing a Caesar salad, we made a startling discovery. The recipe involved a) raw eggs b) ground up stale bread crumbs c) disgusting little fish. Upset with this knowledge, I sliced my hand open and bled into the salad. Worried that the married couples might feel an aversion to cannibalism, we quickly found some mayonnaise, mixed it in, and called it "Thousand Island." Unfortunately, it was the married couples—the wives—who noticed several discrepancies. For one thing, Thousand Island does not go on Caesar salads. Two, they had not packed any ketchup or, for that matter, Thousand Island.

Which accounted for us, the next night, being relegated to washing up. We were under close scrutiny now, and immediately we were accused of shirking even this responsibility. But we weren't shirking, we merely had designs of using nature as our ally. Instead of washing the dinner pots[1] and dishes, we planned to let small rodents clean them during the night. Of course, the argument that followed was nothing compared to one we had the next night, when I started washing the dishes. Well, I really hadn't started to wash them, but I did have them floating in a large eddy. I commented how they all looked like little boats (wine makes me say the damnedest things sometimes) a point agreed to by my fellow bachelors. What quickly followed was a reenactment of Pearl Harbor. Casualties were heavy.

Except for rescuing Spud, we became officially banished from the group, which, for scientific purposes, was good because—with sociology on my mind—I could make the following notes:

- ☞ Married couples do not like eating out of pots and pans with their fingers.
- ☞ Never try to keep up when you're drinking with experts but if you *insist*, always remain out of range of things that could be thrown by married couples.
- ☞ Large quantities of wine and whiskey do not mix.
- ☞ Nor do married couples and bachelors on self-supported kayak trips.
- ☞ Never regurgitate in your sleeping bag.
- ☞ Never go looking for water in the middle of the night without a flashlight unless you know how to find your tent by braille.
- ☞ There are cacti in the desert.

Although we bachelors were blamed for everything that went wrong on the trip—including the trip itself—I myself blame the weather. As we descended the river, the weather had grown progressively colder, a fact the married couples also blamed on us. By the last morning of the trip, our river clothes were so thoroughly frozen they stood of their own accord, and if they had had any sense, they would have walked off and refused to run the rest of the river. At the take-out it was snowing, something All Points was holding me personally accountable for. But she didn't stop there. She continued her tirade until we reached Jordan Valley, where she launched into her finale. In short, I was responsible for everything wrong with the world: past, present, and future.

Later, in the sanctuary of a hamburger joint, I made a last addi-

---

[1] Besides, washed pots never boil.

tion to my notes reminding me to never see All Points again. But fate lusts for irony.

❖ ❖ ❖

Ten years passed. Within that time, the Owhyee, not a place known to breed headlines, managed to dominate the news twice. The first involved a typical genius rafter who, wanting to share the thrills of living off the land, fed his clients poison hemlock.

The second item concerned one Claude Dallas, who, foolishly believing that he *could* exist in the wild without such amenities as McDonald's (while avoiding poison hemlock), attempted living a life of subsistence in the upper reaches of the Owhyee. Two state game cops came to remind him that eating the local deer population was not a suitable substitute for hamburgers, but Claude turned out to be touchy about the subject.

His double-murder case came to trial in Ada County, Idaho, a place not only short on men, but particularly short on *handsome* ones. An all-female jury unhooked Claude on account of his good looks. Which explains both the fairness of the American judicial system and yet one more shortage in Ada County: good optometrists.

Around this time, for no plausible reason, I did the East Fork of the Owhyee, an upper section starting in Nevada. Our party was a mixed group. I was no longer young but, as Carol assured me, I still could act immature.

As we put in, a familiar pattern appeared (although I didn't realize it at the time). The weather was warm and pleasant, and since boats were now smaller, they carried less gear, like the warm clothes we weren't wearing, that we left behind.

By evening, at exactly the time we wanted to camp, it started raining. I don't know who first labeled this country as desert, but the strain of humor wasn't growing on me. Save for the rattlesnakes that came out to dry between the downpours, nothing notable happened other than it grew progressively colder. It was, boringly enough, "a good trip"—until déjà vu struck all over again.

Standing at the take-out was All Points. She and her party had been running another fork and were, due to the rain, now stranded without a shuttle. I had the only truck within thirty miles.

I said I'd do what I could to help, drove two miles, and sat mired up to my axles for twenty-four hours until the road dried out. Of course, All Points thought I'd abandoned them, and she convinced her cohorts I was easily capable of such villainy. When we unfortunately ran into her again in Jordan Valley she orchestrated her group in screaming choruses at me, as if somehow their failed shuttle was my fault. Ironically, it was the same spot where she had reached her last crescendo, ten years before almost to the day.

I mention this incident because it was the reason why I bought a four-wheel drive. Next time, filled with compassion for my fellow man, I could get away from such modern-day Donner wannabes as quickly as possible. Only next time, ten more years later, if I *hadn't* had my four-wheel drive, I wouldn't have gotten in trouble.

The specific trouble was that this time, the truck actually got us to the river. A two-wheel drive would have failed miserably. On this occasion, we were trying another upper section, the South Fork. Our party was just the three of us: Carol, Bill, and myself.

The upper Owyhee country consists of fingered valleys, flat graded hay fields surrounded by nondescript mountains—though not so nondescript that they don't have names. Access to the South Fork is via a long dirt road, where I naturally assumed I'd find old abandoned ranches circa the Depression era. But this was shady-tax-shelter Nevada. For the next twenty-five miles of dirt road there were half a dozen immaculate ranches all painted white, all owned by one outfit. Now, I'm not saying this was a Mafia operation, but whoever owned it sure knew how to swing a good deal on white paint.

Of course, with so much white paint around, we didn't just pass through without permission. This was done at the ranch office, not a place we wanted to approach with L-shaped bulges under our coats. Inside was Ice Station Zero, a secretary so cold that ice cream remained frozen within 50 feet of her. Anyone who had crossed the Berlin Wall would understand the difficulties of getting past such a treacherous obstacle as this one.

Ice Station informed us that since we hadn't made prior arrangements, we couldn't continue. I imagined that we might mess up some secret nocturnal operation, such as a transfer of multiple gallons of white paint from a DC-6 into a fleet of unmarked panel vans. Still, we should have listened to her. Instead we insisted on speaking to the ranch manager. She picked up the phone and began talking to, as I assumed, Mr. Big in the Bahamas.

Ice Station said, "You don't want them to go in there, *do you?*" And, "It is very muddy in there right now and they *really* don't want to go in there *do they?*"

After a long time we received permission, but while waiting we came down with a bad case of hypothermia. As we went out the door, Ice Station allowed us exactly one smile—forced, tight, and evil—as if someone were stretching cellophane over her mouth. I could tell she was looking forward to our communal demise—so long as she didn't have to fill out the paperwork.

We drove past additional white paint and down miles of greasy road consisting more of mud puddle than mud. Occasionally, our shuttle driver, a rancher whom we had picked up in Jordan Valley, would say things like, "Why it's rainin' so hard I can't even see out yer winders." And, "I think you're plum crazy m'self!" And, "Why look there now! It's just a-rainin' like a herd of cows peeing on a flat rock!" and finally, "Why, I jus' *know* yer nuts!"

I had to admit, she had a way with words.[2]

Finally, the road disappeared completely under a mud puddle that was roughly the size of the Pacific Ocean. Our driver dropped us off beside a swollen creek, at a hay shed that, fortunately, was out of sight of the last ranch. Unfortunately, the shed was being used for its intended purpose, meaning we were forced to bivy on top of the stack, with rain pounding on a tin roof that was less than six inches from our eardrums.

For the next forty-two hours we stayed there, shouting at each other. I'm not sure what the Guinness Book lists for bivying on haystacks but, for the record, during that time we never touched the ground. At one point during the first night the pounding of rain stopped, and Bill woke me, yelling in my ear, "Whit! Whit, It's stopped raining!"

"Good," I said filtering the words through my sleeping bag.

"No, it's not. It's snowing."

In the morning we awoke to find Bill gone and the haystack making strange, groaning noises.

"Where do you think he went?" Carol asked.

"MMMMMnnneiiissxxxessxxxxxyyyyzzzz!" said the hay pile.

"What the hell was that?"

"I don't know, but it woke me up this morning."

"$$$$&&&&####%%%%@@@@@!!!!!" said the hay pile once more.

---

2 So did her husband who was supposed to have driven us but as he said, "I just sawed off a couple of ma fingers and now I'm short-handed."

"Sounds like cuss words in a comic strip to me."

"Maybe this hay pile is possessed."

"And with Bill gone, this doesn't look good."

"EEEEELLLLLPPPPP!"

"Huh, sounded like help that time."

"EEEELLLLPPPMMMMEEEEDDDAMMMMNNNIITTT!!!!"

"Look, it's coming out of this crack."

Cautiously shining my light down the rift, I spotted Bill's sleeping bag wiggling like a disturbed grub six bales deep.

"Quick," I said, "get the throw line! It's Bill. He's fallen in a crevasse! I think he's still alive!"

Bill was shaken but otherwise OK. He desperately needed a cup of coffee and so did we, but brewing coffee and accidentally burning down a hay shed belonging to some guy whose name probably ended in O—like Brando, De Niro, Duvallo, Puzo, or Spaghettio— didn't seem like a good idea. We weren't anxious to wake up with horse heads in our sleeping bags.

Time passed in geologic increments. We talked of everything. Even golf.

"It's a stupid sport," Carol said.

"Sure is," Bill agreed.

"Couldn't be any dumber," I said. "Abusing some poor little ball with a stick until it retreats down a hole, then insisting that it come out to take more abuse. It's sick."

"Sounds like something Kafka would have thought of. Who else could have produced such idiocy?" Carol added.

"A Scotsman," Bill said.

We sat there maybe for five minutes saying nothing, watching the snow and the rain, for not only was it doing both now, the stuff was whizzing past us in horizontal streaks.

"You know," Bill finally said, "they play it in the sun."

"Play what in the sun?" I asked.

"Golf."

"So?"

"So, they don't play it in the rain—or snow. They wouldn't be sitting here. They'd be sitting right now in the clubhouse where it would be warm."

"I'd be having a cup of coffee right now," Carol said.

"Not me," Bill said. "I'd be having a gimlet."

"I'd order both," I said.

We sat there shivering some more. I don't know who said it first but we all spontaneously agreed that as soon as this trip was over we were going to take up golf.

During the second night our hay shed floated away. At least Bill thought it had.

"Whit! Wake up!" he yelled. "We're floating away."

"No, we're not."

"Yes, we are. That field we went to sleep by last night is gone and *now* look: We're passing by a lake."

Trying to use reason I said, "Naw, couldn't be. See that wave there in the creek? It was a hole yesterday."

"Yes, but there was a wooden bridge over it. Where's the bridge now?"

"I'm sure it's still in that creek somewhere."

"Yeah, but where did the creek go?"

He had a point. Although I knew he was wrong, I desperately wanted to agree. I was hoping we'd float right on down the river to the take-out without getting wet or any colder than we already were. I let the argument pass.

The next hours were even longer than being on hold and waiting for help from a software technician. Finally, I said, "Looks like it's not raining as hard," and everyone agreed to this lie. It was better than everyone agreeing to "Looks like we'll all be loonytunes if we wait here another minute," which was the truth. In a heroic effort, we quickly chucked our possessions off the stack and, like refugees, jammed them into our boats. On the crest of the flood we fled.

We did twelve miles in two hours and barely dipped our paddles in the water. With all the logs and flotsam in the river it was hard to find a place to dip a paddle in anyway.

Over the following four days, we rode on the diminishing flood. The weather calmed to hail squalls every five minutes and suddenly I found myself dealing with typical river problems, like:

Bill: "You think this is that drop on the map?"

Me: "Either it is or it isn't."

Bill: "By the way, where is the map?"

Me: "I thought you had it, but maybe Carol's got it, that is if I didn't burn it last night."

Bill: "What do you think the weather is going to do now?"

Me: "Looks like we're either going to have rain or snow if this hail ever stops."

Bill: "You know what I like about you? Precise answers."

However, during a brief, pseudo-warming spell, there were also more immediate and less abstract questions to be answered, like:

Carol: "Do you think that poison ivy Bill is standing in will have any effect on him?"

Me: "No, not as much as that coiled rattler he's about to step on."

Really, though, the poison ivy was a blessing. It was nature's way of warning us of impending rapids and portages, since these were the only places it grew—thickest, of course, on the portages.

The flood made for big, interesting water but it didn't help the unimaginative names some rafter had dubbed these drops. Take, for example, "Cabin," or "Cable," or "Devil's Pinball," and for ultimate originality, "Raft Flip." We high-end mensas had better ideas. In keeping with the Hawaiian theme, we went with Pineapple Crusher, Luau Cinder, The Big Kahuna, Five-Uh-Oh, Tiny Bubbles, Larger Bubbles, and Nitrogen Narcosis.

Discussing various routes down one of these drops, Bill commented, "Well, the left looks good, but here comes Carol's boat. Let's see how it manages down the right!"

Carol shrugged as she looked at her boat—along with the prospect of a multi-day walk out. She said, "I don't think this sort of thing ever happens in golf."

I'm positive that golf hazards don't involve falling over thirteen-foot ledges head first—which I did two days later on a portage. In twenty-seven years of boating, this was the only time I had simultaneously needed my life jacket and helmet. With the wind knocked out of me and aching nowhere in particular but all over, I got up and began doing something akin to a rain-dance. Carol peered over, and, as if commenting on the weather I was dancing to, said, "Hey! How'd you get down there so fast?"

Otherwise, in general, the trip was without incident. We froze the entire distance except when we became too numb to notice. At night our gear was soaking, and we could never get adequate fires going for warmth. It wasn't until we were a mile above the take-out that the sun at last broke through, exactly at the time we hit the hot springs. We climbed in and melted. All was right with the world: Then and there I even forgave All Points.

"Golf," I said. "Really is a stupid game."

"Sure is," Bill agreed.

"Whatever made you bring that up?" Carol asked.

Bill, who sought refuge under this hot spring for so long his hair washed off.

Further Reading

Although I have no wish to degrade the following writers, their books were of immense influence in piecing together this book:

In the humor department, the original spark for starting this book I thank especially, Dave Barry. I've enjoyed all of his books. Other writers include Patrick F. McManus, Will Cuppy (*The Decline and Fall of Practically Everybody*), Jerome K. Jerome (*Three Men in a Boat*), and Mark Twain (*Innocents Abroad* and *Roughing It*).

For travelling, my two favorite books to take along are *Don Quixote* and *The Complete Short Stories of Mark Twain*.

A smattering of other books that I've enjoyed:
Barker, Ralph. *The Last Blue Mountain*
Benuzzi, Felice. *No Picnic on Mount Kenya*

Collins, Larry & Lapierre, Dominique *Freedom at Midnight*
De Poncins, Gontran. *Kabloona*
De Saint Exupery, Antoine. *Wind, Sand and Stars*
Elvin, Harold. *The Ride to Chandigarh*
Harrer, Heinrich. *Seven Years in Tibet*
Hornbein, Thomas F. *Everest: The West Ridge*
Hopkirk, Peter. *The Great Game*
Hopkirk, Peter. *Trespassers on the Roof of the World*
Hynes, Samuel. *Flights of Passage*
Jones, William H.S. Jones. *The Cape Horn Breed*
Lansing, Alfred. *Endurance*
Maclean, Fitzroy. *Eastern Approaches*
McGovern, William. *To Lhasa in Disguise*
Markham, Beryl. *West with the Night*
Moitessier, Bernard. *The Long Way*

Moitessier, Bernard. *Sailing to the Reefs*
Moorehead, Alan. *The Blue Nile*
Moorehead, Alan. *The White Nile*
Murphy, Dervla. *Full Tilt*
Nansen, Fridtjof. *Farthest North*
Newby, Eric. *The Last Grain Race*
Newby, Eric. *A Short Walk in the Hindu Kush*
Newby, Eric. *Slowly Down the Ganges*
Salzman, Mark. *Iron and Silk*
Simpson, Joe. *Touching the Void*
Theroux, Paul. *Riding the Iron Rooster*
Thesiger, Wilfred. *Arabian Sands*
Thesiger, Wilfred. *The Marsh Arabs*
Younghusband, Sir Francis. *The Epic of Mount Everest*
Zinsser, Hans. *Rats, Lice and History*

The following books relating to the text may be purchased from these addresses:

- *White Water Nepal* by Peter Knowles and Dave Allardice
  Menasha Ridge Press
  3169 Cahaba Heights Road
  Birmingham, AL 35243

- *Never Turn Back: The Life of Whitewater Pioneer, Walt Blackadar* by Ron Watters
  The Great Rift Press
  1135 East Bonneville Ave.
  Pocatello ID 83201
  $16.95 Postpaid

Available from the Eddie Tern Press
- *Travels with a Kayak* by Whit Deschner $19.95
- *Burning the Iceberg: The Alaskan Fisherman's Novel* by Whit Deschner $12.95
- *How to be a Jerk in Bristol Bay: An Abuser's Guide* by Whit Deschner $9.95

Please include $2.00 for shipping and handling.
The Eddie Tern Press
HCR 88 Box 169
Baker OR 97814

Orders or comments may also be e-mailed to:
whit@pdx.oneworld.com

Which cruise was the better one it is not easy to say.
Each of them had its own log; and the chips from the one
are not like the shavings from the other—except in this,
that they came from a pleasant paddle.

—John MacGregor, *The Rob Boy on the Baltic, 1892*

ABOUT the Author

Whit Deschner

Brevity is the soul of Whit.

—Bill Harzia

Photographer Bill Harzia, Whit Deschner's altered ego, was born several years after both his parents had passed away. He began aimlessly wandering the globe until he reached the Sudd in Africa where, on a fluke, he met Whit Deschner. Currently he resides with his dog, Fillo Dough, in the small principality of Freeloadia where he has his kayak and eats it too—and thinks often about the philosophical meanings of kayak spelt backwards.

DATE DUE

AUG 8 2005		
AUG 29 2005		
SEP 16 2005		
FEB 6 2006		
JAN 3 1 2009		
FEB 1 8 2008		
SEP 2 0 2010		